SAF SHELTON HENRY

THE WIFE PATRICK HENRY KEPT IN THE CELLAR

SHEILA PHELPS INDERBITZEN

outskirtspress

DENVER, COLORADO

Outskirts Press, Inc.
http://www.outskirtspress.com

ISBN: 978-1-4787-6885-2

Outskirts Press and the "OP" logo are trademarks belonging to Outskirts Press, Inc.

PRINTED IN THE UNITED STATES OF AMERICA

ACKNOWLEDGMENT

My sincere gratitude to three Shelton descendants who, with their knowledge and love of the Shelton family, started my path to research deeper into the story of Sarah Shelton Henry and her extended family.

All three of these Shelton descendants truly enjoyed sharing their knowledge with others about Shelton families.

These Sheltons originated from the Norfolk, England, Sheltons: Judge Houstan Dale Shelton, Arkansas county Arkansas; Downing Abbott Bolls Sr, Taylor county Texas; Dr. William A. Shelton, Mecklenberg County, Virginia.

David Valentine Shelton
1789-1864

TABLE OF CONTENTS

Chapter I: Who is Sarah Shelton Henry? 1
Chapter II: The Shelton Ancestral Home, Rural Plains 15
Chapter III: Sarah's Marriage 22
Chapter IV: The New Lawyer 27
Chapter V: William Parks, Virginia's First Editor
                  and Printer (1700-1750) 32
Chapter VI: Shelton (Skelton) Cousins 36
Chapter VII: England Sheltons 39
Chapter VIII: Sir John Shelton (1472-1539)
                  and Lady Anne Boleyn 42
Chapter IX: Martha Henry Fontaine (1755-1818) 45
Chapter X: Anne Henry Roane (1767-1799) 48
Chapter XI: Elizabeth Henry Aylett (1769-1842) 52
Chapter XII: Sarah's Sons: John William and Edward (Neddy) . 58
Chapter XIII: Patrick Henry Fontaine, First Grandson
                  (1775-1852) 62
Chapter XIV: Sarah Shelton Aylett Fontaine (1811-1876) 67
Chapter XV: Philip Aylett Jr. (1791-1848) 77
Chapter XVI: William Winston Fontaine (1834-1917) 80
Chapter XVII: Patrick Henry Fontaine (1841-1915) 84
Chapter XVIII: Sarah Fontaine Redd (1815-1909) 89
Chapter IXX: Spencer Roane Thorpe (1842-1902) 92
Chapter XX: David Shelton (1736-1800) 94
Chapter XXI: Some Nephews and Great-Nephews 97
Chapter XXII: Anges Shelton Sutherland (1757-1821) 113
Chapter XXIII: David V. Shelton's Rebel Hill,
                  Buffalo Springs, Virginia 116
Chapter XXIV: The Grave 122

INTRODUCTION

This is a story of revolutionary war patriot Patrick Henry's first wife, Sarah Shelton (1738-1775). This woman was confined to the cellar of her home by her husband, Patrick Henry. Sarah Shelton Henry was thought to be insane or possessed by the devil.

Today, Sarah Shelton Henry would probably be diagnosed as suffering from postpartum depression or puerperal psychosis. Those are two types of illnesses that sometimes affect women after the birth of the child. Sarah Henry's mental state of mind did begin to decline after the birth of her last child. In fact, a letter written to Patrick Henry's sister from their mother stated, "We feel Sarah is losing her mind after the birth of little Neddy."

The Henry family did have a private doctor, Dr. Hinde, who suggested to Patrick Henry that his wife be sent to the new hospital in Williamsburg. This new hospital was twenty miles away from the Henry home. The doctor felt that Sarah could be cared for by people that were experienced in handling people like Sarah—at least, that's what he thought.

Years after the death of Dr. Hinde, his son found some notes of his father's. Some of these notes made reference to what Dr. Hinde had seen on one of his visits to Scotchtown, the Henry family home. Dr. Hinde described what he had seen in the cellar of the Henry home. Not only did he find Sarah Shelton Henry confined to the cellar, but she was also wearing a "Quaker dress."

This would probably be what we know today as a medical

straitjacket, something that would prevent the person from possibly harming themselves or others. I would think that Sarah Shelton Henry was probably restrained a number of times in that Quaker dress. I do not know if Dr. Hinde made any reference to a trapdoor leading to the cellar where Sarah was kept, as has been suggested by a number of references.

Whether Sarah Shelton Henry was insane or not is something that will never be known, because Patrick Henry did not leave many documents about his life before becoming governor of Virginia, or about his first wife, Sarah Shelton. Little is known about the Henrys during the time they lived at Scotchtown in Hanover County, Virginia. This secret way of life was kept from the people of Virginia.

Most people of Virginia did not know what the Henry family had to endure day after day for three to four years. This dark secret could never be exposed—the dark secret of having your wife living her life in the cellar. These were very politically active years for Patrick Henry. He was trying to make a change for Virginia and was also becoming the first governor.

He could never let anyone know that his wife, Sarah, was thought to be insane or possibly possessed by the devil. During the colonial times in America those types of situations were never talked about—not outside the family, at least. I would think families that had to deal with such a heartbreaking situation did all they could to do with what resources they had. I'm sure those families that were put in that situation did not know what to do. They did not even know what it was that had changed their loved one.

I'm sure Mr. Henry felt that no one could know that the woman he loved had been taken away from her children, from him, and from the life she knew before. Possibly, Patrick Henry's hard work and determination was driven by the fact that he wanted so desperately to help his loving wife, Sarah, but did not know how.

After Sarah Shelton Henry's death, Patrick Henry became the first governor of Virginia, married a woman as young as his daughter, and sold their family home, Scotchtown. One of Sarah and Patrick Henry's sons was in love and wanted to marry Dorothea Dandridge, the woman would later become the new Mrs. Henry, but Dorothea Dandridge, or her father, chose the governor of Virginia over his son. This son suffered from a very deep depression that was thought to be because the woman he wanted to marry married his father. References suggest he never fully recovered from his depression.

The cellar floor at Scotchtown, where Sarah Shelton Henry was kept, was thought to have been dirt at the time of Sarah's confinement. There were no cobblestones on the cellar floor at that time. There was major renovation done to the house by new owners in 1802 and then again about 1832, and no one really knows if there were any windows in the cellar at the time the Henrys occupied Scotchtown. I would think that if there were no windows at the time Henry bought the house then there would have been no windows in the cellar when he sold it. One of Sarah Shelton Henry's brothers visited Scotchtown at the time the Henry's lived there. He described Scotchtown as being, "The plainest of sort," with only the necessities. I'm sure that was the case, because with the master of the plantation gone most of the time and the mistress locked in the cellar then there was no need for nothing but necessities.

On one of my visits to Scotchtown, the staff did confirm that there had been a trapdoor, but at some point in history someone had made a closet and had enclosed the area. This would have been not far after entering what is now considered the back entrance to the house, which would have been in the area where the Henry family ate their meals. This would have been away from the main part of the house.

Since Patrick Henry was away from his home so much he asked his newly married daughter, Martha, and his son-in-law, John Fontaine, to live at Scotchtown. Henry wanted Martha to help care for her mother and her younger brother and sisters, and he wanted his son-in-law to run the plantation. They say Henry did have a female slave that stayed with Sarah Henry in the cellar. Scotchtown tells the story that this female slave stayed in the room that joins the room where Sarah was confined. There is an entrance on the east side of the house that will take you down some steps to the room where his female slave stayed.

Years after the Henry family left Scotchtown there was a kitchen attached to that side of the house. That structure was torn down many years ago. What remains now is probably much as it was when the Henry family was there.

The Fontaines did move to Scotchtown with Patrick Henry. Martha Henry Fontaine played an active role in her father's political life. Martha Henry Fontaine had at least one child while living at Scotchtown.

If Sarah Shelton Henry did suffer from postpartum depression or puerperal psychosis she must have lived a miserable, lonely life in that cold, damp, dreary dungeon of a cellar. This woman was taken away from everything she had known before and put in a place not to live but to die. Sarah Shelton Henry did not deserve to live or die in a cellar. Maybe she should have been confined to another part of the house, possibly a bedroom where she could have been more comfortable. They could have still bolted her door where she could not have wandered off.

Maybe living upstairs would have been more comfortable for Sarah, but more disturbing for her family

And what is so sad is that no one knows where Sarah Shelton Henry is buried, because Patrick Henry did not leave anything to let the world know where he had buried his wife. In recent years, speculation has been that Sarah Henry is buried in an unmarked grave thirty feet from the cellar at Scotchtown

In the past few years there was an archaeology team that went to Scotchtown to examine the area thought to be the unmarked grave of Sarah. This unmarked grave was thought to be under a huge lilac bush close to the cellar. I do not know where the archaeologist obtained his information to search in that area.

A few months after the archaeology team conducted their research I called Scotchtown to obtain the results of their findings. I was told that they did find a grave and it was a female. I was also told that without any further research they could not confirm it was Sarah Shelton Henry. I was told by Scotchtown that for the archaeology team to continue their research they would have to possibly uproot or severely damage the old lilac bush, because the grave was under the lilac bush.

I do not believe that either Scotchtown or the state of Virginia wanted to disturb the old lilac bush. I was also told during that conversation that no other research would be done on this found, unmarked grave. Scotchtown said its focus was on the house itself.

In late summer of 2012, I visited Scotchtown again. On that visit I asked about the unmarked grave that was found by the archaeology team. Some staff members said there was no grave found and one staff member said one was found but they did not want to search any further. I'm not sure why there has been conflicting information on the archaeology team's findings.

But the fact still remains that no one really knows where Sarah Shelton Henry is buried, because Patrick Henry did not leave much information about his life while at Scotchtown. Research suggests that Patrick Henry never spoke of Sarah after her death, I guess, because of all of the sorrow and pain. Such a heavy burden was put on that fairly young man and his family.

The Sheltons of Hanover County Virginia were a very respected family in colonial times. Sarah Shelton was born and raised in the Shelton family home, Rural Plains. The Shelton home was built by Sarah's great grandfather, John Shelton of Lancaster and Westmoreland County, Virginia. Rural Plains has always been owned by a direct male descendant until 2006.

Sarah Shelton's ancestors go back to the reign of King Henry VIII and his wife, Queen Anne Boleyn. The Sheltons played an important role in Henry VIII's court. Sir John Shelton was master of the household, and his wife, Lady Anne Boleyn Shelton, was an aunt of Queen Anne's and was the governess of the future Queen Mary. Later, she was governess to Elizabeth I. After Elizabeth became Queen of England she brought the Sheltons back to court.

Sarah Shelton's maternal grandfather was William Parks. William Parks was Virginia's first printer. He also established Virginia's first newspaper, the Virginia Gazette. Sarah's grandfather also owned the Hanover Tavern and Inn and the land across the road where the Hanover Courthouse would later be built.

Sarah Shelton Henry's parents would sometimes leave their home, Rural Plains, and live at the Hanover Tavern and Inn for a while. Sarah, Patrick, and her family lived at the inn for at least two years when their first home burned. The fire destroyed their farm of three hundred acres that Sarah's father had given them when she married. Their farm was called Pine Slash.

The Henry family lived with the Sheltons in Hanover County until Patrick Henry could find something he was good at. He had not been very successful at their farm. With Henry being unskilled in labor, and with only six slaves and a drought, their crop was a disaster. Sarah's father, John Shelton, supported the Henry family until Patrick could find something to do.

I am a direct descendant of Sarah's brother, David Shelton, of

Hanover County, Virginia, and Caswell County, North Carolina. I write this book to show that there was more to Sarah Shelton than just "the wife of." This woman's life and death should be acknowledged. Sarah Shelton Henry has a wonderful story to be told. She at least deserves that.

Maybe women that experience the feelings that Sarah may have felt after the birth of a child need someone to listen to them. Maybe no one wanted to listen to Sarah Shelton Henry.

No names, family names, locations, or events mentioned in this book show any disrespect to any family or any of their descendants.

This book is written to show respect and to honor a woman that history has either forgotten or has never acknowledged.

I
WHO IS SARAH SHELTON HENRY?

Sarah Shelton was the first wife of Revolutionary War patriot Patrick Henry. She was a woman who obviously suffered from what we know today as postpartum depression or puerperal psychosis. It was an illness that affected this woman for three to four years, until her death.

To my knowledge, Sarah Shelton Henry has never been recognized as much more than the daughter of a Hanover County, Virginia, farmer, and the first wife of Patrick Henry. There was so much more to this woman than that, and her father, John Shelton, was more than a farmer. There is so much history to Sarah's life, her family, her extended family, and her English ancestors.

While researching my mother's family, the Sheltons of Hanover and Mecklenburg County, Virginia, I discovered Sarah. My mother's cousin, a retired Arkansas county Judge, Houstan Dale Shelton, gave me copies of a number of documents that he had, as well as notes from our direct descendant's Bible. The Bible had belonged to David Valentine Shelton, and the Bible was passed on to one of his sons, Dr. John B. Shelton. Dr. John B. Shelton is my great-great-grandfather.

Research shows that Sarah was a beautiful woman, a woman with dark hair and dark eyes. She was referred to by Patrick Henry's mother as a "sweet girl." Sarah was a sister of my direct descendant, David Shelton (1736-1800). There has always been the story passed down through generations of Sarah Shelton who married Patrick Henry, and also the story of Patrick Henry keeping his wife in the cellar of their home.

Some years ago, my aunt, Delores Shelton, told me some stories that she had heard being talked about at some Shelton reunions when she was younger. She said the stories mostly came from her great aunt, Ida Shelton Abbott. Ida was a daughter of Dr. John B. Shelton. My uncle, John Lawrence Shelton, was also interested in the Shelton history. He did get to visit the Shelton ancestral home, Rural Plains, in the late 1960s.

As I began researching Sarah before Patrick Henry and her life after she married him, I found that every book I picked up about Patrick Henry only made reference to Sarah as his "insane wife." I have never found more than two or three statements documented about her. Some have written that Henry had to feed his insane wife after entering the cellar through a trapdoor.

Sarah Shelton Henry must have undoubtedly suffered from postpartum depression or an illness very similar to that. Sarah Henry began to show signs of the illness shortly after the birth of her last child, Edward. They would call him Neddy. Sarah Henry did have a private doctor, Dr. Thomas Hinde, who strongly suggested to Patrick Henry that his wife be sent to the new hospital in Williamsburg. I do not know how long Sarah had been living in the cellar before Dr. Hinde made that suggestion, but for some reason, Henry made the decision to keep his wife, Sarah, at their home, Scotchtown.

In a letter that Patrick Henry's mother wrote to her daughter, she stated, "We feel Sarah is losing her mind after the birth of little Neddy." If Sarah Shelton Henry did suffer from postpartum depression, or any mental illness, then I would think confining her to the cellar to live out her life possibly could lead to insanity.

Since there has never been anything documented, to my knowledge, about those years in the cellar, how do we know Sarah Henry was insane? But then again, if she was suffering from any kind of mental illness, being locked up and away from everybody—children, family, and the whole world—then yes, she probably was insane at the time of her death.

Some years after the death of Dr. Hinde, his son found some of his father's notes, and they stated that on a visit to Scotchtown, not only did he find Sarah Henry in the cellar, but she was wearing a "Quaker dress." This is probably what we know today as a medical straitjacket.

Patrick Henry was very politically active during the years his wife was living in the cellar of their home. I do wonder why Henry did not choose the new hospital in Williamsburg for Sarah. I guess it was because the conditions there were probably unbearable. I wonder if Henry was trying to make her life somewhat tolerable, or was it possibly for fear of embarrassment that his wife might be declared insane? Again, these were very active years for Henry. Patrick Henry was trying to make a change for the colony of Virginia. He was also working on becoming Virginia's first governor.

I can not imagine what thoughts must have been running through Sarah's mind when she realized where she was and what her husband had done. Even if Sarah was suffering from some type of mental illness, there had to be times that she had some rational thoughts and feelings, because women who do suffer from postpartum depression are not insane. If Sarah Shelton

Sarah Shelton Henry
1738-1775

Dr. Hinde

Henry was insane at the time of her death, I feel it was due to her confinement in that one room with a dirt floor and away from the life she had once known.

Research shows that Sarah Henry did have a female slave that stayed with her in the cellar. I would hope that Sarah was treated as if she was living upstairs. I have visited Scotchtown, the home of Sarah Shelton and Patrick Henry. The house is original and has a few pieces that belonged to the Henry family. There is an original cradle that was in the children's room on one of my visits. There was a bedspread or bed cover that was laying across a bed in what was Henry's bedroom; it was thought to have been made by Henry's sister. There was also a tea set in a drawing room next to Henry's bedroom that was given to Henry by his mother.

There are rows of cedar trees that line the walkway going to the front of the house, and the old boxwoods in the front of the house may look as they did so many years ago. Maybe some boxwoods were there when Sarah Shelton Henry was still mistress of Scotchtown.

The house has a full English cellar. If you enter the cellar on the far west side of the house it will take you directly to what the Henry family used as a cold storage room. Then you enter a room where the wines and liquors were kept. In the next room is where the weaving was done. There is a very deep well-like structure lined with cobblestones that is a few feet from the back of the house. This would have been where meats and other very perishable items would have been kept.

If you enter the cellar from the east side and walk down a few steps it will take you to a room where the female slave that cared for Sarah Henry stayed. There is a doorway in this room that connects to the room where Sarah was kept. I'm sure there was a door there at the time Sarah Henry was confined to the cellar.

Sarah's room is somewhat small but it does have a fireplace and now has windows across one wall. No one really knows if the windows were there at the time the Henrys occupied the house; there was extensive renovation done to the house in the early 1800s after the Sheppard family brought the property.

Many, many years after the Henrys left Scotchtown there was a kitchen added to the east side of the house. There are also pictures that were taken sometime, possibly at the time the state bought Scotchtown. One of the pictures not only shows the added kitchen but also shows a small entrance to the cellar from the front of the house.

Patrick Henry was a feisty youth who would roam though the woods with not much more than the thought of hunting or fishing, and his parents would worry about what they thought to be a strange and rustic way of living. Henry did enjoy reading, but did not attend school after the age of fifteen. His rustic appearance did not change till the age of twenty-four. When Sarah Shelton first met Henry, she observed his rustic appearance.

Cellar Window

Doorway to Sarah's Room

Entrance to Sarah's Room

Sarah Shelton Henry did have a brother who visited Scotchtown and he described it as, "Having the plainest of sort and only that of necessities." I do not know if this visit was before Sarah was put in the cellar or afterward, but with the master of the plantation gone most of the time and the mistress locked in the cellar then I'm sure Patrick Henry was not thinking about much more than necessities. His thoughts were probably only on his sick wife and making a change for the colony. I would think if the cellar floor was dirt during the years the Henry family owned Scotchtown then I would think it was dirt when Henry sold the house.

With Henry gone so much he asked his newly married daughter, Martha, and his new son-inlaw, John Fontaine, to move to Scotchtown. He wanted Martha to help care for her mother and the younger children; he wanted John Fontaine to manage the plantation. Having only been married a couple of months, the Fontaines left their farm and moved to Scotchtown.

If Sarah Shelton Henry did have any sense of what was going on in the world above her tiny room, I could only imagine how disturbing her thoughts may have been to know there was no way out of the situation—not physically or mentally.

While Sarah's daughter, Martha, was at Scotchtown, she did care for her younger brother and sisters while the female slave stayed with her mother. I would like to think that Martha also cared for her mother.

I would think Sarah probably knew very shortly after being sent to the cellar that she would never be able to escape the life that the cellar brought. She probably knew that the life she had known before was gone—no more children, no more family, nothing as she knew before. And she probably also knew that her husband was the one that had put her in the cellar to live out her life. She probably also knew her husband's ways and knew he would never change his mind and reconsider her living upstairs again with her family. I'm sure she took those thoughts to her grave.

Patrick Henry had already sold most of the slaves from Sarah's marriage dowry. Henry had sold the slaves during the time he was failing at everything he was trying to do. I do not know where it is documented that there was a female slave who stayed with Sarah Shelton Henry. Scotchtown, the home of Sarah Shelton and Patrick Henry, tells the story that there was a female slave.

Patrick Henry left very few documents during the time the Henry's were living at Scotchtown. He also never documented where he had buried Sarah. Sarah is like the flowers of spring that stay dormant for a while and then break the soil to let us know of their existence.

Patrick Henry was a great orator and a man who did change the colony of Virginia, so we do need to know who Sarah Shelton Henry was, because without her and her family who knows what path Patrick Henry may have taken.

Although the new hospital in Williamsburg was suggested by Sarah's doctor, it probably would not have been a good choice for Sarah Henry, because like all the others there, I'm sure she would have been chained to the wall or possibly a bed. I'm sure Patrick Henry struggled with what to do with his ill wife—someone that, I'm sure, had changed into someone he may not have even known. Someone that maybe was not that dear, sweet girl he had married, but someone that was a stranger to him, someone that he didn't understand what she was thinking or what she was doing.

I'm sure Sarah Henry's door was bolted at all times, and if she did display bursts of outrages then they probably did wrap her body with cotton or linen to restrain her. How sad. Here, this woman was taken away from her family and her children, not only to live in the cellar, but also to die there. If Sarah was restrained she would have had no contact with her children.

Sarah's children would have ranged from one year of age to sixteen when she was sent to the cellar—this is assuming that she was sent there the same year as the birth of her last child. This would have been in 1771, and if it was postpartum depression then it would have been in that first year.

I wonder if Patrick Henry had thought of putting Sarah in one of the upstairs bedrooms. He could have still bolted the door so she could not wander around the house or outside. But, Scotchtown is a one-story house, so maybe Henry was afraid to have Sarah so close, because again, these were very busy, busy months and years for Henry. I'm sure there were people coming and going that he was trying to impress in some way.

The Henry family had a dark secret that they had to keep from the people of Virginia. So, I guess, Henry felt like putting Sarah in the cellar was the best choice.

By this time Patrick Henry was already a lawyer and was not having to depend on his father-inlaw, John Shelton, to support his family. Sarah's father and her mother, Eleanor Parks, had supported the Henry family for a while. The Henrys had lived at the Shelton Tavern and Inn until Patrick Henry could find something that he was good at. Sarah's mother had inherited the property and Tavern when Sarah's grandfather, William Parks, died. Sarah's grandfather was Virginia's first newspaper editor.

The cellar that Sarah was forced to live in must have been a cold, damp place in the winter, and Sarah was there at least three winters. On each of my visits to Scotchtown, I would always feel such a strong sadness and loneliness each time I entered Sarah's room. I would look around the room at the fireplace and the cobblestones that now line the floor and think, "This is like a high-class dungeon." I could not imagine what it may have looked like two hundred plus years ago with only a dirt floor beneath her feet.

Sarah Shelton Henry did not get to live in the governor's mansion with her family. She died in the spring of 1775 in the cellar where she had been living for three to four years, and she has obviously been left in an unmarked grave somewhere. Some speculate the grave is thirty feet from the cellar door, but no one really knows where Sarah Shelton Henry was buried.

To my knowledge no one has ever discovered were Patrick Henry buried his first wife and the mother of his first six children. Patrick Henry did not leave many documents about his first wife or first children while they were living at Scotchtown in Hanover County, Virginia.

So, there, Sarah Shelton Henry was left somewhere in an unmarked grave while her husband and her children went on to a new life—a new life in the governor's mansion with her husband's new young wife. This new wife was a friend of the Henrys' daughter, Martha.

Scotchtown

Scotchtown

Front of Scotchtown

Back of Scotchtown

Entrance to Cellar

II
THE SHELTON ANCESTRAL HOME, RURAL PLAINS

There is no question that Sarah Shelton's life before she became ill was filled with love and happiness. She was born and raised at the Shelton family's home, Rural Plains, in Hanover County, Virginia. The home was built by Sarah's great-grandfather, John Shelton the first. The Shelton home has always been thought to have been built around 1670, but recent studies of the house show it was built a few years later. Sarah's great-grandfather was living at his plantation, Currioman, in Westmoreland County, Virginia, when he built Rural Plains. The Shelton family home in Hanover County, Virginia, stayed in the Shelton family for over three hundred years.

The Shelton home, Rural Plains, has thirteen rooms. The two-story home has an English cellar; the house also has an Elizabethan-style front porch. The floor is made of pine with 10 by 12 inch hewn sills. The house has always been furnished beautifully. There is a four-poster bed that was brought from England in 1635 from the Shelton Castle. The bed was listed in the Domesday Book in the Eleventh century. I don't know who was in possession of the bed before it was brought to Rural Plains.

The bed was said to have been used by Queen Elizabeth I when she lived in the Hatfield house with the Shelton family. This was before it was taken to the Shelton Castle in Norfolk, England. The fireplace at the Shelton home, Rural Plains, carries memories, also. This is were Sarah Shelton married Patrick Henry in 1754.

The mantle over the fireplace in the front room is original. It's made of heart of pine. The floors on the first floor have been replaced, but the ones on the second floor are original.

Some of the bricks on the outside walls were imported from England. The walls in the cellar are three-feet thick. In the attic the beams are marked with Roman numerals and were also imported from England.

John Shelton the first originally had five thousand acres with his Rural Plains home.

During the Civil War there was a lot of activity at the Shelton home. General John Hancock and his union troops took over Rural Plains for a while. They used what is now the front room as their Union Hospital. General John Hancock used the Shelton house for his head-quarters. General Hancock had wanted the Sheltons to leave their home, but because someone in the family was sick they refused to go and stayed in the cellar until the Union troops left.

A number of years ago I got to visit Rural Plains. Mr. William Shelton was not home at the time I was there, but I did have a won-derful talk with Mrs. Shelton. She told me I could walk around the grounds and take as many pictures as I liked. She also invited me to come back later when Mr. Shelton was home. She said he would love to talk with me since my mother's family was descended from the Hanover County, Virginia, Sheltons.

At one time the Shelton family home housed hundreds of histori-cal pieces that were probably all owned by a Shelton. Guns, muskets, a Revolutionary War helmet, paintings, swords, furniture, quilts, and many, many other pieces were part of a Shelton family who lived at Rural Plains. Mr. William Shelton was the last owner of Rural Plains.

Shelton House
Rural Plains

Rural Plains

In 2001 Mr. William Shelton donated the Shelton home and the remaining 125 acres to the Richmond National Battlefield Park. Mr. Shelton did not have any children.

In 2006, Mr. William Shelton died and Richmond National Battlefield Park took possession of the Shelton home, Rural Plains, and the remaining acreage.

There has been continuous work being done to preserve the home and the land. There had never been any type of archaeology work done at Rural Plains, but in 2008 an archaeology team uncovered what was thought to be the original kitchen and slaves quarters there at the Shelton home. The remains that were unearthed were to the west of the main house. The back of the house faces west.

More than three hundred years later, the Shelton house is still as grand as it ever was. It has been the home of many Sheltons and their families. I am sure, like so many other grand houses, that it has had many happy times and many sad times. There have been many Sheltons who were born and died in the home, as well as many, many parties and weddings. There has also been evidence of wars on this Shelton land.

One of those wars was in May of 1864, when Union troops invaded the Shelton home and advised Mrs. Shelton, wife of Colonel Edwin Shelton, that she and her family would have to leave Rural Plains. They told Mrs. Shelton that there would soon be a battle on her plantation. She refused to leave her home. Mrs. Shelton and her family stayed in the cellar until the battle was over. Her husband, Colonel Shelton, and his troops were across the creek waiting for the battle to begin.

There is so much history there at the Shelton home. After Mr. William Shelton's death there were numerous boxes and trunks found in the attic. These trunks contained many, many artifacts that in time will help us to understand more about the many Shelton families that lived in that wonderful house in the last three hundred years.

Rural Plains
Back of Rural Plains

Dec 6 1970

Staff Photos by Don Pennell

Mrs. W. R. Shelton Jr. Holds Old Quilt
Bed Was Named in Domesday Book of 1086

Mrs. Robert Shelton
1970

Family Home in Hanover Boasts 300-Year Tenancy

By Louise Ellyson

In the 10 years of her marriage, Mrs. William R. Shelton Jr. has yet to find time to catalogue all of the books in her house, Rural Plains. Moreover, she is constantly digging up metal objects like a lock or farming equipment in the garden.

The Hanover County house has an unusual, if not unique, history in Virginia in that Shelton represents the ninth generation of Sheltons to live there since its completion about 1670, hence the vast collection of memorabilia both indoors and out.

(The children of Mr. and Mrs. C. Hill Carter Jr. at Shirley Plantation are the tenth generation there but the present house was built early in the 18th century. An-

Richmond Newspaper
Dec 1970

III
SARAH'S MARRIAGE

Sarah Shelton was sixteen when she married eighteen-year-old Patrick Henry. That was in October, 1754. They married in the front parlor of the Shelton family home, Rural Plains. Neither the Sheltons nor the Henrys were very excited about the marriage. It wasn't that the Henrys did not approve of Sarah, because they did. They found her quite the dear, and sweet. Their concern was that their son, Patrick, was just too young for marriage, and also I'm sure there was a concern about their son not really having any kind of employment at all. Patrick Henry's father wanted his sons to do well in business. Patrick was working behind the counter at a merchant's store at fifteen years old. The next year, Patrick Henry went into business with an older brother. The business did not do well at all. At the time of the marriage, I don't believe Henry was working at all. I've never found anything to confirm he was.

But the parents of the young couple finally gave their approval and the marriage took place. Sarah's father, John Shelton, gave the couple a farm called Pine Slash. The farm consisted of three hundred acres. Along with the farm, he gave them six slaves. Farming was not something that Patrick Henry was very good at. Although there were slaves to help, Henry being unskilled in labor made it very difficult. The Henrys tried growing tobacco, but that failed. There was a terrible drought that year, so the tobacco crop was a disaster. During those few years at Pine Slash, Sarah gave birth to two children: Martha (some articles referred to her as Patsy) in 1755, and John in 1757. That was a busy year for the Henrys—all within that one year Sarah gave birth to a son, her home and farm were destroyed by fire, and she had to move back in with her parents.

The next few years Sarah and her family mostly lived with her parents at the Hanover Tavern and Inn. Henry decided to try the merchandising business again. This business only lasted a few years. It left him bankrupt, and by this time, he didn't have many friends left.

Sarah's mother, Eleanor, had inherited the Hanover Tavern and Inn from her father, William Parks, Virginia's first newspaper editor. William Parks had established a newspaper in Annapolis, Maryland, before establishing the Virginia Gazette in Williamsburg. William Parks established a paper mill on a branch of the Archer's Hope Creek in 1744. Mr. Parks had donated the land across from the tavern to build the Hanover Courthouse.

Patrick Henry worked for his father-in-law, John Shelton, probably on a part-time basis. Living and working at the tavern gave Henry the opportunity to go to the courthouse and talk politics with other men. That's something Henry enjoyed very much, talking. I guess as the years went on his talking skills improved.

I wonder what type of marriage Sarah Shelton Henry really had. All that we know is that her troubles seemed to begin shortly after her marriage. Her troubles started with the burning of her first home, her husband not being able to provide for his family for a number of years, and her terrible illness, which began shortly after the birth of her last child.

And, with Patrick Henry being gone so much here, there, and everywhere, who knows if there was even any romance in their marriage. I believe Henry probably concentrated more on making a name for himself and making changes for Virginia than possibly thinking of romance.

As hard as it was on Sarah with all she had to deal with, I hope the marriage was one of love. If the love was there then I'm sure it made the heavy burden that was put on them a lot eaiser.

Hanover Tavern

Second floor of the Hanover Tavern
1988

Back of Tavern
1988

Hanover Tavern

Barksdale Theater

IV

THE NEW LAWYER

When all else failed, Henry decided to try law. He did love to read and talk, so he probably thought, "I can become a lawyer!" The Henry family was still living at the tavern in Hanover when Henry decided to try his hand at another adventure. Since the merchandising business and farming was a disaster, I guess that was a good choice for Henry. And what was also nice was that the Hanover Courthouse was directly across the road from the tavern where he lived with his in-laws.

I wonder what Sarah Henry was thinking when Patrick told her he was going to try law. After all, nothing had really worked out since their marriage—and really even before. Sarah probably thought, "Well, you do like to talk and be around people, so maybe you can do it." I'm sure Sarah remembered how Patrick would just close the store and walk over to the tavern or courthouse just to talk to people. Who knows whether Sarah was supportive of her husband's decision to practice law or not, but I do know that many people felt that he could not do it. And, as far as John Shelton, Henry's father-in-law, was concerned, he probably felt like Henry should just do something that he was good at so he could support his family.

Resources say that Henry studied law for only six weeks. That's what he told Thomas Jefferson, anyway. George Wythe accepted Thomas Jefferson as his law student, which lasted five years. Thomas Jefferson was nineteen years old when he began studying under Mr. Wythe.

Mr. Wythe refused to sign Henry's law license. Mr. Wythe felt Henry had not had the proper training to become a lawyer. Patrick Henry's license to practice law was later signed by someone else. He was twenty-four years old. But then it was another three years before a case came up that Henry could handle.

Henry would work in the tavern, especially when Sarah's father was away on business or going to the family home, Rural Plains.

Patrick Henry

Hanover Virginia
Courthouse

Hanover Courthouse

Henry's first big break in law came when he worked on the "Parson's Clause." Henry was very stong-willed and spoke with great confidence—and, maybe it didn't hurt that his father was the presiding judge that day.

Patrick Henry was not the first choice for his position as a burgess. Someone had to resign and a position was created for Patrick Henry. But, as the years went on, Patrick Henry became a very successful lawyer, and a lot of great things came his way—all the way to the governor's mansion.

I am sorry that his wife, Sarah Shelton, did not get to share in some of his success. It would have been nice for Sarah to get to enjoy a part of Henry that maybe she never knew. But, because of her death, she was left probably there at Scotchtown in an unmarked grave while her husband and children made a new life in Williamsburg in the governor's mansion. Patrick Henry was elected the first governor of Virginia in 1776.

Hanover Courthouse

Hanover Virginia
Old Jail

V

WILLIAM PARKS, VIRGINIA'S FIRST EDITOR AND PRINTER (1700-1750)

Mr. Parks was Sarah Shelton Henry's maternal grandfather. He was born in Shropshire, England. Before arriving in the colonies, Mr. Parks had printing offices in Ludlow, Reading, and Hereford. He had published the Ludlow Post-Man in 1719 while living in Ludlow. Mr. Parks had become an established printer while still living in England.

Through my research I only found two children born to William Parks and his wife, Eleanor—a son, and a daughter also named Eleanor, who was the mother of Sarah Shelton Henry. Eleanor, the daughter, was born after arriving in the colony of Maryland.

Mr. Parks began printing documents in the Maryland colony in 1726, and in 1727 he began printing government documents. By 1728 he was printing for the Virginia colony. His business was quite successful in both colonies. As early as 1729, William Parks went back to England to purchase some printing tools for his Williamsburg office. His printing business in Williamsburg was such a success that in 1734 he closed his Annapolis, Maryland, office and moved to Williamsburg. He concentrated solely on that office, and by August of 1736 he had printed the first Virginia Gazette.

The Virginia Gazette was a weekly paper. Mr. Parks was also a book publisher. He would purchase books from England that were in single sheet form. He would bind them together into a book for each individual customer. He would also publish books from Virginia authors. At some point, Mr. Parks was the postmaster in Williamsburg.

In the spring of 1744, since his business was doing so well, Mr. Parks decided to build a paper mill on Archer's Hope Creek, not far from Williamsburg. But, the mill began to produce a poor quality of paper, so Mr. Parks discontinued the mill operation.

Mr. Parks had accumulated a lot of land in what is now Hanover County, Virginia. He had built a tavern and inn on the main road from Richmond to Williamsburg, and he also owned the land that the Hanover County Courthouse sits on. The tavern and courthouse still stand. The tavern has had many owners; what is now the back of the tavern was originally the front. At some point in history, when they stopped using the old road, they made the front entrance face the courthouse.

When Mr. Parks died, his estate was left to Sarah Shelton Henry's mother, Eleanor Parks Shelton. After Mr. Parks's death, the Sheltons closed up their country home, Rural Plains, for a while and lived at what they called The Hanover Tavern. Sarah Shelton and Patrick Henry lived at the tavern for a while after their first house burned.

On March 23, 1750, William Parks was on the ship, Nelson, on his way back to England to purchase more printing supplies. He developed pleurisy and died on April 1. He was buried in Gosport, England. Mr. Parks' original Williamsburg printing office burned in the 1890s. At a later date, a building was built on the lot and was called Williamsburg Printing Office. William Parks also left a large estate in Maryland and land in New Castle, Virginia.

Sarah Shelton Henry's maternal grandfather, William Parks,

contributed a lot to the Virginia colony. His Virginia Gazette continued to be published in Williamsburg till April 8, 1780. At that time, the newspaper was moved to Richmond, which had become the new capital of Virginia.

Hanover Tavern

Compleat COLLECTION

OF THE

LAWS of Maryland.

WITH

An INDEX, and Marginal Notes, directing to the several Laws, and the chief Matters contained in them.

Collected and Printed by AUTHORITY.

William Parks
Printer

VI
SHELTON (SKELTON) COUSINS

By 1764, Sarah and her three children and Henry had moved to Louisa County, Virginia. While living at her father's tavern in Hanover, she had another son, William. William was born in 1763. William later became sheriff of Craven County, North Carolina, and served till his death in 1794. William died without children.

John, Sarah's second child, died when he was a young adult. He was a captain in the Revolutionary War. John suffered from a deep depression that some say was brought on by his father's second marriage. John was also in love with Dorothea Dandridge, but the first governor of Virginia, his father, Patrick Henry, won her hand in marriage.

The Henry plantation in Louisa County was named Roundabout. Sarah had another daughter, Anne, who was born in 1767 while living at Roundabout.

Sarah Shelton Henry had many, many cousins; most of them lived in the surrounding counties of Goochland, Hanover and Louisa.

One of Sarah's distant cousins was Bathurst Shelton [Skelton]. The son of James Shelton and Jane Meriwether, Bathurst was born a little later than Sarah. He attended William and Mary along with Thomas Jefferson. Bathurst and Thomas were both interested in the hand of marriage of Miss Martha Wayles. Miss Wayles was the daughter of John Wayles of Charles City County, Virginia. Bathurst Shelton and

Miss Wayles did marry. Bathurst Shelton and Martha Wayles lived on land called Elk Island in Goochland County, Virginia.

Research shows that the couple only had one child, John. When Bathurst Shelton (Skelton) died in 1766, Martha and the child moved back to her father's plantation, The Forest. Mr. Wayles was a lawyer with a large fortune. Mr. Wayles had married into money. He married Martha Epps. She had brought a large dowry with her, which included many, many slaves. Martha Wayles Shelton stayed at her father's plantation until she married Thomas Jefferson.

Jefferson had high social status, but needed a lady with him that also had social status. Martha was beautiful and would bring a large dowry of property upon the marriage. The couple married in January of 1772. When Martha's father died in 1774, Jefferson's slave holdings tripled.

Among the slaves were Betty Hemings and her daughter, Sally Hemings. Sally's father was John Wayles. Research shows that Mr. Wayles fathered a number of Betty Hemings' children. I don't imagine that Martha Wayles Jefferson knew that Sally Hemings was her half-sister, and probably never imagined that years later Sally, her half-sister, would win the heart of her husband, Thomas Jefferson.

Martha Wayles Jefferson never fully recovered from the birth of her last child. Martha died in September of 1782 and is buried in the family cemetery with three of her children. It is said that Thomas Jefferson was so sick with grief over the death of his wife that he stayed in his room for weeks.

Edmund Bacon, who was the overseer at Monticello at that time of Mrs. Jefferson's death, told the story that Betty Hemings was the one that cared for Mrs. Jefferson until she died.

The story of Thomas Jefferson's romance with his slave, Sally Hemings, had been rumored for years, but in 1802 the rumor went to the press. Recent DNA studies have confirmed that Sally Hemings' last son was fathered by Thomas Jefferson, and other DNA studies strongly suggest that Mr. Jefferson was also the father of Sally Hemings' other children.

Some research shows that other distant cousins of Sarah Shelton Henry were Joseph Shelton and Major Thomas Shelton. Their two portraits are at Scotchtown, which were at one time on loan from the Shelton home, Rural Plains. There is another portrait that was in the children's room of Mary Massy Shelton, daughter of Major Thomas Shelton, and his first wife, Cecilia Darby. Other research shows that Joseph Shelton and Major Thomas Shelton were uncles of Sarah Shelton Henry.

There are many cousins of Sarah Shelton Henry that played a very active role in American history.

VII
ENGLAND SHELTONS

Any spelling is still the present day Shelton. Sarah Shelton Henry's Shelton line descended from the Norfolk house in Norfolk, England. Their name was taken from the village of Shelton in Norfolk.

Sir John Shelton, born around 1280, had succeeded to the Norfolk and Suffolk estates. He first married a Maud, and then a Hawys, daughter of the Prince of Powys of Wales. This was all passed down to his son, Sir John Shelton, who was born in 1300, and his wife, Agatha.

In Cumberland, England, Sir John had Skelton-Shelton Castle. This castle was later passed on to his son, Ralph (1315-1378). This Ralph became lord of the manor at eighteen years of age. This Sir Ralph definitely made his name throughout history. Documents indicate he was at the Battle of Crecy in the king's company. He was knighted there for helping save the Black Prince. The Black Prince was Edward the third. This Sir Ralph Shelton married Anne Burgulion, daughter of his cousin, Sir Ralph Burgulion. After Sir Ralph Burgulion's death, Ralph Shelton became heir to Great Snoring Estate in Suffolk. This Ralph Shelton later married Joan dePlais of Wetyng.

The same Ralph Shelton built old Shelton Hall, a castle surrounded by a moat. He also built St. Mary's church at Shelton. Both Shelton and his wife are buried at St. Mary's. The original tombs were life-size and made of bronze. By 1606 Shelton Hall was near destruction. The same coat of arms used by this Ralph Shelton was later used by the

Sheltons of Hanover County, Virginia.

Later in history, Sir Ralph Shelton, born in 1426, married Margaret Clere, who gave birth to a son, Sir John Shelton (14- 1539). Both father and son were mentioned in a number of history books. This Sir John was High Sherriff of Norfolk in 1504 and was knighted in 1509. He was Knight of the Bath at the coronation of King Henry VIII. This Sir John Shelton was married to Lady Anne Boleyn Shelton (14-1556). She was an aunt of Queen Anne Boleyn. Both Sir John Shelton and his wife, Lady Shelton, played an active role in King Henry VIII's court as well as Elizabeth I's court.

Ralph Shelton (1560-1628) was married to Jane West. One of their sons, James (1590-1668) came to America with his uncle, Sir Thomas West, in 1610. This James was later known as James the first. He was living in Jamestown, Virginia, in 1620. His descendants were in Lancaster, Westmoreland, Hanover, Goochland, and Louisa counties, Virginia.

The Sheltons definitely have their place in history, from the years before the Norman Conquest to the first Shelton arriving in America in 1610, and all the Sheltons that were to follow.

Jamestown, Va.

The James River

VIII
SIR JOHN SHELTON (1472-1539) AND LADY ANNE BOLEYN

This Shelton and his wife, Lady Anne Boleyn Shelton, played a very active role in the years of King Henry VIII and Elizabeth I. Shelton married Lady Anne Boleyn, daughter of Sir William Boleyn of Blicking, Wiltshire, and Margart Boteler. Lady Anne Boleyn Shelton was an aunt of Queen Anne Boleyn.

Sir John and Lady Shelton first lived at Shelton, Norfolk, England. Later, the Sheltons lived at court during King Henry's reign. Sir John Shelton was governor of the household, and some history books refer to him as being steward or master of the household. King Henry VIII must have liked and approved of Shelton, because in later years the king gave the grant of Carrow Abbey to Shelton. After years of the abbey passing down through family members, the abbey was bought in 1871 by a private firm. There was still Shelton glass in the abbey when it was purchased.

In this Sir John Shelton's earlier years, he was High Sheriff of Norfolk and was knighted in 1509. He was present as a Knight of the Bath at the coronation of Henry VIII.

Lady Anne Boleyn Shelton was governess to the Princess Mary, who would become Queen Mary. As the years went on, so did the roles of the Sheltons. In the time of Queen Mary's reign, when the future Queen Elizabeth I was treated so badly by her half-sister, Queen Mary,

Elizabeth went to live with the Sheltons. Later, when Elizabeth I became queen of England, she sent for the Sheltons to live in the palace in London.

Lady Margaret Bryon was assigned to Elizabeth when she was born because Lady Shelton was still governess to Mary. Shortly after Elizabeth I was born, the king sent her to live at Hatfield. That became her residence. While Elizabeth was still an infant, King Henry sent orders that Mary was also to be sent to Hatfield to live. When the Sheltons arrived at Hatfield, Lady Shelton continued to be in charge of Mary, and Sir John Shelton became master of the household at Hatfield. The king and queen would rarely ever visit Mary or Elizabeth.

Lady Bryon and Sir John Shelton did not agree on many things. One thing was that Lady Bryon wanted Elizabeth to eat in her own apartment and John Shelton thought she should eat in the dining hall.

One of the Shelton's sons, also Sir John, and his wife, Margaret Parker, lived in the royal court during Elizabeth I's entire reign. One of Sir John and Lady Anne Shelton's daughters, Margaret (Madge), seemed to be one of King Henry's infatuations. Madge was not only a cousin of Queen Anne Boleyn, but also an attendant in the queen's court. Madge later married Sir Thomas Wodehouse of Kimberly, Norfolk.

After Elizabeth I became queen of England, the Shelton family stayed in her court until the queen's death in 1603.

From these Sheltons, the American line of Sheltons began with James Shelton (1590-1668). James Shelton's parents were Sir Ralph Shelton and Jane West. Jane West's grandmother, Katherine Carey, is said to be the illegitimate daughter of King Henry VIII and Mary Boleyn. The king and Mary had an affair before the king and Anne Boleyn married.

Blickling Hall
Norfolk, England

Norfolk, England

IX
MARTHA HENRY FONTAINE
(1755-1818)

Martha was the first child of Sarah Shelton and Patrick Henry. She married her second cousin, John Fontaine, when she was eighteen years old. John Fontaine had been mostly raised at his parents' plantation, Rock Castle, near the Pamunkey River. The couple married on October 2, 1773, at Scotchtown. The Fontaines only lived on their farm for a few months before moving to Scotchtown. Sarah had undoubtedly come to a very critical stage in her illness. With Patrick Henry gone so much of the time and with Sarah locked in the cellar there was no one to care for the younger children. Henry probably had a female slave to watch over the younger children and Sarah, but if he had sold all of Sarah's slaves, as some research shows, then there may have only been Martha to care for her mother most of the time. No one really knows for sure; so much is only speculation.

And after all, Patrick Henry was keeping a dark secret. I would think there were only a very few people who knew Henry's wife was being kept in the cellar of their home, and I would think these were only family members and close friends of the family. I'm sure the people of Richmond, Williamsburg, and Philadelphia did not know this. There would be no way that Henry would have wanted this family secret to reach the people of Virginia. Only a short time before Sarah's death did some people know of this.

One of Sarah Henry's brothers had visited Scotchtown, but I don't know if Sarah was living in the cellar at that time or not. When the brother visited Scotchtown and found all of the things to be plain was probably after Sarah was living in the cellar and Martha was there with the children. Martha was young and newly married and probably had a heavy burden put upon her by her father. With Patrick Henry gone most of the time, that only left Martha and her new husband to take care of everything, including the children and also the running the entire plantation. The young couple was probably unskilled in any labor, which made the burden heavier.

Martha and her husband did stay at Scotchtown until Sarah died in the spring of 1775. After Sarah's death, Martha and her family continued living at Scotchtown for a while. In the latter part of 1776. Patrick Henry was elected governor of Virginia. Then, later, he married a friend of Martha's. The Fontaines went with Henry to Williamsburg and later to Richmond. Martha would serve as hostess for her father. In 1778, the Fontaines bought some land on Leatherwood Creek. Later, Patrick Henry gave the rest of the property to his daughter and son-in-law. They stayed there for a while before buying a home in Prince Edward County, close to Henry and his new wife and children. They called their home Locust Grove. But, in 1791, the Fontaines moved back to Leatherwood. Martha's husband, John Fontaine, had contacted malaria while at the battle of Yorktown and never fully recovered. They thought moving back to Leatherwood would improve his health, but it did not. Sarah Shelton and Patrick Henry's son-in-law died in 1792.

Martha Henry Fontaine had seven children. Her oldest child was Patrick Henry Fontaine (1775-1852). He was the first grandson of Sarah Shelton Henry. He was born the same year that Sarah died. In later years, he moved to Mississippi. He was the land surveyor of the Chickasaw Indian land in Mississippi. He was at his grandfather's side when Patrick Henry died at his home, Redhill.

Martha Henry Fontaine had another son, William Winston Fontaine (1786-1816). He was born at the Leatherwood plantation in Henry County, Virginia, but he was raised at Locust Grove plantation. He was a land surveyor like his father. William married Martha Hale Dandridge and had three children before his death.

In 1816 he traveled by horseback to northern Alabama to look at some land to possibly purchase. This area of Alabama had good land and was fairly cheap. When he finished exploring the area, he and his slave started traveling back to Virginia when they ran into a bad storm. It rained for days. Mr. Fontaine and his slave made camp around the Abington, Virginia, area. William Winston Fontaine died at the campsite from pneumonia. The slave buried his master beside the creek bank near their campsite. His slave took Mr. Fontaine's horse and his belongings back to his plantation. His slave told the family where he had buried his master. Mr. Fontaine's widow was twenty-one and was left with three small children to raise.

Martha Hale Dandridge Fontaine died in 1875 at one of her grandson's homes in Reidsville, North Carolina.

Reverend John James Fontaine (1788-1852) was another son of Martha Henry Fontaine. He married Mary Carr Redd and lived in the Redd family home Belleville. Belleville was built by Mary's grandfather, John Redd. Many Fontaines and Redds intermarried. John Redd was one of the first settlers in Henry County, Virginia.

In 1802, Martha Henry Fontaine sold a thousand acres of her Leatherwood plantation and lived on the remaining thousand acres until her death in 1818. The burial site of the Leatherwood plantation cemetery, where Martha Henry and her husband John Fontaine are buried, is now a paved parking lot, like so many historical sites.

X

ANNE HENRY ROANE
(1767-1799)

Anne was the second daughter of Sarah Shelton Henry. Anne was born while the Henry family was living at their Roundabout plantation in Louisa County, Virginia. Anne was only eight years old when her mother, Sarah Shelton Henry, died, and was still very young when Patrick Henry married his second wife, Dorothea Dandridge.

Dorothea Dandridge was about the same age as Anne's older sister, Martha. As the years went on, Dorothea Henry felt like the family should move to Richmond, so Anne and her younger sister, Elizabeth, would have a much better chance of finding a more suitable husband. Patrick Henry must have agreed with Dorothea, because the Henry family did move to Richmond, Virginia.

Anne later met Spencer Roane. He was working as an aide to the governor of Virginia, Patrick Henry. But, before Anne Henry could marry Spencer Roane, he wanted to make sure that his future wife would have an equal part in Mr. Henry's estate upon his death. Spencer Roane had written a letter to Patrick Henry asking him to put in writing that all of his daughters would have an equal part in the estate, but Mr. Henry did not want to do that and did not.

But, Patrick Henry did agree to meet with Mr. Roane about this matter. There was a verbal agreement made between Mr. Henry and Mr. Roane. Mr. Henry agreed that all of his daughters would have an equal share of his estate.

This same request was made by Philip Aylett before his marriage to Anne's younger sister, Elizabeth.

Anne Henry and Spencer Roane were married on September 7, 1786, at Salisburg, the Henry home in Chesterfield County, Virginia. Patrick Henry was renting the home from Thomas Mann Randolph at the time of Anne's wedding.

Anne Henry and Mr. Roane had seven children: four sons and three daughters. They lived at the Roane's family home, Mahockney, in Essex County, Virginia.

Spencer Roane was appointed judge of the court of appeals in 1794. Mr. Roane would later be judge of the supreme court in Virginia.

Anne Henry Roane's first child, William Henry Roane (1787-1845), was very politically active, like his father. He was a member of the Virginia House of Delegates, Democrat of the Virginia State Senate, and later was chairman of the Committee of the District of Columbia. After his political career, Mr. Roane moved to Tree Hill, Virginia. He died in 1845 and is buried in the Lyons cemetery in Hanover County, Virginia.

In 1794, after Spencer Roane was appointed judge, he sold his family plantation, Mahockney, and moved to Mount Clement on the Tappahanneck-Richmond road.

Anne Henry Roane died May 20, 1799. She died at her sister Elizabeth's home in King William County, Virginia. Anne Henry Roane is buried in the Aylett cemetery at the old Aylett plantation at Fairfield.

Spencer Roane wrote a letter to Patrick Henry dated May 24, 1799. This letter was to advise Mr. Henry of the death of his daughter, Anne. But when the letter was received at Redhill, the plantation where Patrick Henry and his second family were living, the family did not give the letter to Mr. Henry. Mr. Henry was too ill and the family felt it would be too much for him.

The letter stated, "The cup of my misery, my dear sir, is now full, by the loss of my most amiable, virtuous, and affectionate consort, your dutiful and affectionate daughter."

I do not know if the family ever told Patrick Henry about the death of his daughter, Anne, before his death.

Later, Spencer Roane filed a complaint with the court contesting Patrick Henry's will. It was against the executor of the will, Patrick Henry's wife, Dorothea Dandridge Henry. This complaint was filed on behalf of Spencer Roane's deceased wife, Anne Henry Roane. In the complaint it stated, "That there was considerable danger of the children of Patrick Henry's first marriage being unjustly dealt by through the influence of his then wife, the present defendant, Dorothea Henry."

In Patrick Henry's will, he willed to Anne and Elizabeth, daughters of Sarah Shelton Henry, two hundred pounds each, "As soon as my estate can conveniently pay it by cropping", and five hundred pounds to be paid to Anne, Elizabeth, and older daughter Martha. Patrick Henry did not will any property of any kind to any of Sarah Shelton Henry's daughters.

Spencer Roane, husband of Anne Henry, had a very successful political life. After Anne Henry's death, Mr. Roane remarried in 1801. Mr. Roane and his new family later moved to Richmond, Virginia.

Spencer Roane died in 1822 and is buried in Warm Springs, Virginia.

Spencer Roane
1762- 1822

William Henry Roane
1787- 1845

XI
ELIZABETH HENRY AYLETT
(1769-1842)

Elizabeth, or Betsy, as she was called, was the fifth child of Sarah Shelton and Patrick Henry. She married Phillip Aylett and was the mother of thirteen children. Elizabeth was said to have favored Sarah more than any other of her other children. She had long, raven-black hair and dark eyes. A painting done of Elizabeth when she was young, and then another painting done when she was older, showed characteristics of someone that would have been tall with a slender frame. She did have a nose like her father, long and slender. She was a beautiful woman, and what paintings I have seen of some of her children and grandchildren, they were also attractive.

Elizabeth was only six years old when her mother, Sarah Shelton Henry, died. Being so young, she probably never really knew her mother, because Sarah was confined to the cellar at least three years before her death. So, that would have made Elizabeth only three when her mother was sent to the cellar; it is very possible that Elizabeth never saw her mother after the age of three.

Elizabeth Henry Aylett's father, Patrick Henry, married a year or two after Sarah's death. So, Elizabeth could have possibly been close to Patrick Henry's second wife. That wife was considerably younger than Patrick Henry. In fact she was very close to the age of Elizabeth's older sister, Martha Henry Fontaine.

Patrick Henry's new wife wanted to make sure that Elizabeth and her older sister Anne married good and well-to-do gentleman. When Dorothea Dandridge introduced Elizabeth to Philip Aylett, Elizabeth was either extremely nervous or did not approve; Elizabeth pretended to faint. Later, Dorothea told Philip that Elizabeth was just nervous during all the excitement of meeting him.

Patrick Henry's new wife had wanted the family to move to Richmond so Anne and Elizebeth could find a good and well-to-do gentleman to marry. Both sisters did find and marry good men.

Elizabeth Henry married Philip Aylett at St. John's Church in Richmond on October 12, 1786. The Aylett's lived at the family home, Fairfield, for a few years before moving to their plantation, which was called Montville, also in King William County, Virginia. The land was part of the original tract of the Fairfield plantation. The house is still standing and can be seen from the main road. Over the years there were additions added to the house. It was the home of many generations of Ayletts.

However, before Philip Aylett married Miss Henry, Mr.Aylett's guardian wanted to make sure that Elizebeth's father, Patrick Henry, would provide a sufficient dowry. Elizabeth was seventeen and was ready to marry Mr. Aylett, but before that could happen, Philip's guardian wanted to make sure that Miss Elizabeth would have an equal share in Mr. Henry's estate upon his death. This guardian of Mr. Aylett's wanted Patrick Henry to put it in writing, but Patrick Henry refused. It is said that Mr. Henry did not want to write a fixed sum. Patrick Henry told Mr. Aylett that he would give all his daughters an equal share, but would not put it in writing.

It seems that Patrick Henry and his second wife, Dorothea, were living a higher standard of life in Richmond than Mr. Henry's pocketbook could stand. Henry was financially having a hard time; a letter that Patrick Henry wrote to Elizabeth later confirms that.

And while all of this was happening, Spencer Roane, who would later marry Elizabeth's older sister, Anne, was also asking Patrick Henry to put in writing Anne's dowry. Spencer Roane wanted to make sure his future wife would also get an equal share of Mr. Henry's estate.

Patrick Henry did not put anything in writing, but he did meet with Mr. Roane and with Philip Aylett's guardian.

Elizabeth Henry Aylett had thirteen children, and she outlived all but two: a son, Philip Aylett Jr., and her youngest daughter, Sarah Shelton Aylett Fontaine.

Elizabeth Aylett died at her daughter's home, Fontainbleau, also in King William County, Virginia. Elizabeth died September 14, 1842. I don't know how long Elizabeth had been living with her daughter. She is buried in the Aylett cemetery at Fairfield.

In 1989, the old Aylett cemetery was discovered and restored by the King William County Historical Society. Photographs, after being restored, show two large trees at the entrance of the old cemetery. There is a brick wall that surrounds the cemetery.

Elizabeth Henry Aylett left many, many descendants that were very successful in their lives—descendants that Sarah Shelton Henry would have been very proud of.

Elizabeth Henry Aylett
1769- 1842

Elizabeth Henry Aylett

Aylett Home

XII
SARAH'S SONS: JOHN WILLIAM AND EDWARD (NEDDY)

John was the second child born to Sarah Shelton Henry, and was her first son. He was also born at Pine Slash in Hanover County, Virginia, like his sister, Martha Henry Fontaine. The Henry family lived on their farm, Pine Slash, until the house burned and they had to move in with his grandparents, the Sheltons, at their Hanover Tavern and Inn in the town of Hanover.

The Henry family lived with the Sheltons for a few years. John's father, Patrick Henry, would help John Shelton at the Tavern and Inn until Patrick Henry could find a way of supporting his family. The Sheltons would spend most of their time in the town of Hanover, except when they would go to their family home, Rural Plains.

John Henry's childhood was also spent in Louisa County at the Henry's family home, Roundabout.

John was a soldier in the Revolutionary War. He served as captain of the first continental artillery. Research shows that John Henry (1757-1791) suffered from deep depression, which some thought was brought on by the many deaths of John's soldiers. But, research also shows that John may have suffered this deep depression from the fact that his father, Patrick Henry, married the girl that John was in love with, Dorothea Dandridge.

Dorothea Dandridge was a friend of John Henry's sister, Martha

Henry Fontaine. Martha, John, and Dorothea were all about the same age. It must have been devastating for John when he found out his father was to marry the girl he loved. Dorothea Dandridge was nineteen years younger than John's father, Patrick Henry.

I wonder what type of relationship John Henry and his father had after Patrick Henry married Dorothea—I would think a strained relationship. Research shows that John Henry suffered this deep depression until his death. John later married a Susannah Walker. Miss Walker was also born in Hanover County. The Henrys had one child, Edmund, who was born July 1791. Edmund Henry, son of John, lived most of his life in Perry County, Iowa, in the township of Red Rock.

Edmund married a Nancy Williams and had two sons. Edmund Henry died in 1855 and is buried in the Pleasant Hill cemetery in Perry County, Iowa.

John first son of Sarah Shelton died in Henry county, Virginia. John was buried at the Leatherwood plantation. His wife, Susannah, remarried in 1798 and died in Abington, Virginia.

William was the second son and the third child of Sarah Shelton Henry. There is not much known about William Henry (1763-1798).

Again, Patrick Henry did not leave much information about his first wife and family. William did marry, but did not have children. He married a woman that was much older than he. She was said to be a wealthy widow that was born in Rhode Island. They were married in 1787. William was twenty-four when they married.

William was the sheriff of Craven County, North Carolina, from 1794 until his death in 1798. My fourth great-grandfather, David Shelton (1736- 1800), was an uncle of William Henry. David Shelton was a brother of William's mother, Sarah Shelton Henry.

David Shelton was also a sheriff. He was the first sheriff of Caswell County, North Carolina. David Shelton held other positions in Caswell

County before his death.

In William Henry's will, he left most of his estate to his wife, Elizabeth Graves Cooke Henry. He left his widow land in Hanover County Virginia, and ten thousand acres in Norfolk County, Virginia.

It is unknown where Sarah Shelton Henry's son, William, is buried. His wife, Elizabeth, lived a number of years after William's death. She left part of her estate to her sister, Mary Graves Bright. It is also unknown where Elizabeth is buried. Both are possibly buried in what is now the New Bern, North Carolina, area.

Edward (Neddy) as he was called, was Sarah's third son and her last child. He was born in 1771 at the Henry's plantation, Scotchtown, in Hanover County, Virginia. Research shows that Sarah's mental health began to decline shortly after the birth of Neddy. There are no records to confirm exactly when Sarah's mental health started to deline , but records were found confirming that it was very soon after Neddy's birth. One of the strongest pieces of evidence to confirm this is the letter that Patrick Henry's mother wrote to her daughter, which said, "We feel Sarah is losing her mind after the birth of little Neddy."

Neddy had studied to be a lawyer. One reason was because he was in love with his first cousin, Sally Buchanan Campbell, and wanted to marry. She was the daughter of General William Campbell and his wife, Elizabeth Henry Campbell. Elizebeth was a sister of Patrick Henry. Patrick Henry wanted his son to be a self-made man before he married.

Neddy was to obtain his license to practice law in February of 1793, but he was too late. Sally married General Frances Preston in January of that same year.

Patrick Henry knew this was a big disappointment and heartache for his son, so Henry gave Neddy 949 acres near his sister, Martha Henry Fontaine.

Edward (Neddy) Henry died in 1794. Some research shows that Neddy is probably buried at Henry's last home, Redhill. But, the Patrick Henry National Museum at Redhill says that Neddy Henry is buried at Winton, in Amherst County, Virginia. Winton was the family plantation home where Neddy's aunt, Jane Henry Meridth, lived. Neddy possibly moved to the Amherst, Virginia, area to practice law.

All three of Sarah Shelton Henry's sons died at a fairly young age, and Edward (Neddy) probably never saw his mother, because Sarah became sick when Neddy was very, very young. Hopefully, Neddy's older sister, Martha Henry Fontaine, told him some good and loving things about their mother, Sarah, and some things about their life before their mother became sick.

XIII
PATRICK HENRY FONTAINE, FIRST GRANDSON (1775-1852)

Patrick Henry Fontaine was the first grandson of Sarah Shelton and Patrick Henry. He had to have been born at the Henry plantation, Scotchtown, because his parents, Martha Henry and John Fontaine, were living there. Martha was helping to care for her mother, Sarah, and John Fontaine was running the plantation. Sarah Shelton Henry probably had been living in the cellar at least three years before her grandson was born. Patrick Henry was gone most of the time so I'm sure he needed all the help he could get. I'm sure everyone at the plantation did their part to help.

I'm sure Sarah Shelton Henry never saw her grandson, because his birth was just weeks before Sarah's death—this is assuming that Sarah died in the spring of 1775, as references indicate.

Patrick Henry Fontaine's parents, Martha and John, were married in October of 1773 at Scotchtown. I would think that Sarah Henry did not attend the wedding. I'm sure she was already confined to the cellar out of sight from everyone.

Patrick Henry Fontaine was raised at his parents' plantation, Leatherwood. The Leatherwood plantation originally consisted of ten thousand acres. Patrick Henry and his first cousin, Colonel George Waller, and his wife, Ann Winston Carr, had originally bought the ten thousand acres, but later sold some to the Fontaines and had also later gave some of the tract to Martha.

At one time all three families—the Henrys, the Wallers, and the Fontaines—all lived on the ten thousand acres. The plantation also owned one hundred slaves total between the three families. Later, Patrick Henry and his new family moved to Prince Edward County, Virginia. Their farm was called Locust Grove. It sat on Buffalo Creek.

Patrick Henry Fontaine and his family later moved to Greenwood, also in Henry County. The Fontaines lived at Greenwood for a number of years before moving to Pontotoc, Mississippi, where Mr. Fontaine was the chief surveyor for the Chickasaw lands in Mississippi.

While still living in Henry County, Virginia, Patrick Henry Fontaine's grandfather, Patrick Henry, became ill. Patrick Henry's daugher, Martha Fontaine, had received a letter from Patrick Henry advising her he was ill. Patrick Henry Fontaine, his mother, and other family members traveled to Redhill, where Patrick Henry was living. References say that when the family arrived they found Patrick Henry sitting in an armchair.

Dr. Cabell, who was Patrick Henry's physician and friend, told him that the only thing to do was to administer liquid mercury. He advised Mr. Henry that the mercury would either cure him or kill him. Dr. Cabell was so sick with grief that he left his friend and went outside. Dr. Cabell wept for his dear friend.

When Dr. Cabell returned and entered Mr. Henry's room he found Mr. Henry praying. Patrick Henry then drank the mercury. With Patrick Henry's family and his grandson, Patrick Henry Fontaine, all around him, he took his last breath. Patrick Henry died on June 6, 1799.

Patrick Henry Fontaine married Nancy Dabney Miller. They had six children, all being born in Henry County, Virginia. When Patrick Henry Fontaine and his family moved to Pontotoc, Mississippi, there were a number of other family members who also moved. One was his sister, Martha Henry Fontaine, and her husband, Nathaniel West Dandridge.

Patrick Henry Fontaine was the chief surveyor for the Chickasaw lands for a number of years before his death. Patrick Henry Fontaine died at his home, which was called Ridgeway. He died in October of 1852. He is buried in the city cemetery in Pontotoc, Mississippi.

In Mr. Fontaine's will he left his home, Ridgeway, to his daughter, Louisa, after the death of his wife, Nancy. He left his old violin and walking cane to his son, Edward. The walking cane had been given to Mr. Fontaine by his first cousin, William Henry Roane. The cane had belonged to William Henry Roane's father, Judge Spencer Roane. Judge Roane was married to Anne Henry, sister of Mr. Fontaine's mother, Martha.

Patrick Henry Fontaine
1775-1852

Patrick Henry Fontaine's plantation, Ridgeway, was said to be the ideal plantation. Mr. Fontaine was an expert in agriculture, gardening, and breeding of cattle. His wife, Nancy, was very active in the daily operation of the plantation. The original land deed consisted of 159 acres.

Martha Henry Fontaine Dandridge, granddaughter of Sarah Shelton Henry and sister of Patrick Henry Fontaine, also lived in Pontatoc and raised a large family there. One of her daughters, Martha Lightfoot Dandridge, married Richard Bolton. Mr. Bolton was a land agent for the county. The Boltons lived at the Bolton plantation. The name of the plantation was later changed to Rosalba.

One of Patrick Henry Fontaine's sons, Edward (1814-1884), was a very adventurous and interesting person. He was a great-grandson of Sarah Shelton Henry. He was a minister and a teacher, had a law degree, was a draftsman for the Chickasaw land, and was very active in his travels. He also served as captain of Company H, Eighteenth Regiment of the Mississippi Volunteers during the Civil War.

Edward first married Mary Ann Swisher and had children. After the death of his first wife, he married Susan Britton Taylor. Edward, like his father, Patrick Henry Fontaine, also led a very good life.

Edward Fontaine died at his home, Belvedere, in Pocahontas, Mississippi.

Edward Fontaine's first son, Lamar Fontaine (1841-1921), was born in Washington County, Texas. He was educated in Austin, Texas, and at a military academy in Bastrop, Texas. Lamar Fontaine was a great-great-grandson of Sarah Shelton Henry. Lamar was named after a friend of his father's, General Mirabeau Lamar.

When Lamar Fontaine was ten years old he was captured by Comanche Indians. He lived with the Indians for five years before he escaped. He traveled by foot until he reached his home.

Lamar Fontaine enlisted in the Civil War. He later transferred to his father's company in the Army of the Potomac. Mr. Fontaine was in many battles. One of his first injuries was when his horse was killed and he suffered from a broken thigh. Before they could get him off of the battlefield, he was injured again. He was shot in the hip and hit by a Minie ball in the neck.

The neck injury caused Mr. Fontaine to be partly paralyzed in his right arm. After weeks in the hospital in Charlottesville, Virginia, Mr. Fontaine returned to duty and took part in twenty-seven battles during his military career. He had many more battle scars before the war was over.

While still in the Civil War, Lamar Fontaine wrote the poem, "All Quite Along the Potomac." After the war he became a Texas Ranger. He married Liemuella Smith Brickell in 1866 in Yazoo City, Mississippi. Miss Brickell was born in Holly Springs, Mississippi. Lamar Fontaine had eight children. Two of his sons, Edward and James, were civil engineers like their father.

The Fontaines lived in the village of Lyons just north of Clarksdale, Mississippi. At the time of Mr. Fontaine's death in 1921 he was living with a daughter in Lyons, Mississippi. Lamar Fontaine is buried in the Lagrange cemetery in Clarksdale, Mississippi.

XIV
SARAH SHELTON AYLETT FONTAINE (1811-1876)

There are a lot of interesting stories of Sarah Shelton Henry's descendants, but one of my favorites is the one about Sarah Shelton Aylett and her husband, William Spotswood Fontaine. Sarah Shelton Aylett was a granddaughter of Sarah. She was born June 24, 1811 at her family home, Montville, in King William County, Virginia. Her parents were Philip Aylett and Elizabeth Henry. Her grandparents were Patrick Henry and Sarah Shelton. Sarah Aylett lived a comfortable life in the little village of Aylett. There was a distant cousin of her father who would come to Montville to visit. This distant cousin was William Spotswood Fontaine. They were cousins on Mr. Fontaine's mother's side, and Elizabeth Henry Aylett was Mr. Fontaine's great aunt.

On one of his visits, Mr. Fontaine began courting Sarah Aylett. Mr. Fontaine was born November 7, 1810 in Hanover County, Virginia. He was born at the Yellow House plantation of his grandfather, Dandridge. But, as a very young child, his family moved to southern Henry County, Virginia. William Spotswood Fontaine attended the Patrick Henry Academy.

Before Mr. Fontaine married Sarah Aylett he studied medicine under Dr. Honeyman in Hanover County, but he later decided the study of medicine was not something he wanted to continue.

Sarah Shelton Aylett married Mr. Fontaine on July 5, 1832, at her home, Montville. Mr. Fontaine had purchased five hundreds acres of land which already had a hundred-year-old house on the property. The Fontaines lived in the old house until their new home was completed three years later.

The Fontaines named their beautiful plantation Fontainebleau. While living in the old house, Sarah had two children: Elizabeth Spotswood Fontaine and William Winston Fontaine. Elizabeth was born on June 28, 1833, but died that same day. William Winston Fontaine lived to an old age and had a very successful life.

Mr. Fontaine worked very hard in making his plantation, Fontainebleau, as has been described "a model farm"—and it was. He spent many hours studying scientific journals and experimenting with new farming techniques. Mr. Fontaine had created his model farm. The Fontaine family had many visitors, not only from Virginia, but other places as well. They all came to Fontainebleau to admire this beautiful plantation. Their plantation had beautiful trees, hedges, and flowers.

In 1836 Sarah gave birth to another son, Alexander Spotswood Fontaine. This son would only live a few hours. In 1838 Sarah Fontaine gave birth to her third son, Charles De La Boulay Fontaine. But, sorrow came again with the death of Charles in 1856. He died of typhoid fever while attending the University of Virginia in Charlottesville.

Sarah's husband, William, became interested in the improvement of livestock. References say that Mr. Fontaine spent ten thousand dollars to build a barn and storage for his livestock. Mr. Fontaine continued his interest in livestock as well as serving two terms in the state legislature.

On May 19, 1840, the Fontaines had another daughter, Marion Dandridge Fontaine. Marion would later marry her cousin, John. Hairston Redd. Mr. Redd was a physician. Marian was married by her father, who had been ordained into the Baptist Church in the 1850s.

When the Civil War started, everything in the Fontaine family changed. By 1863, all three of Sarah's sons had enlisted in the Confederate Army. Her son, Philip Aylett Fontaine (1845-1862) had enlisted in 1861. Sarah never saw her son, Philip, again. He also died of typhoid fever in 1862 and is buried in one of the flower gardens at Fontainebleau.

As the Civil War continued, more sorrow and grief fell upon the Fontaine family.

In July 1863 federal troops made camp on the Fontaine's beautiful plantation, Fontainebleau. These federal troops destroyed the entire plantation. They destroyed the crops, killed all the livestock except what the troops could eat, and burned all the barns, outbuildings, and everything else standing, except for the main house—everything. Some of the men in the troops made their way to the main house, destroying pictures, Mr. Fontaine's wonderful library, and most of the furniture. At one point, some of the federal troops made a large pile of furniture debris, poured kerosene on the debris, and were ready to burn the furniture when another federal officer walked in and put a stop to the terrible act.

Sarah's husband, William, was not at the plantation when the federal troops destroyed their home. Mr. Fontaine was visiting his sick mother, and Sarah's two surviving sons were in the Confederate Army. This only left Sarah and her two daughters, Marian and Sarah.

In the kerosene soaked debris were family portraits of the Aylett and Fontaine families. Most of these portraits were over a hundred years old. Among the rubble was a picture of Sarah Aylett Fontaine's grandfather, Patrick Henry. One of the female slaves of Sarah Fontaine walked up to one of the officers and asked for the picture. She told the officer that her mistress was the granddaughter of Patrick Henry. At first, he didn't believe her, but later handed the picture to the female slave they referred to as Aunt Rachel.

William Spotswood Fontaine
and
Sarah Shelton Aylett

Fontainebleau

Dependency

The federal troops built large fires on the plantation to cook some of the animals they had killed. They raided the Fontaine's cellar of their liquors and wines. This raid of fourteen thousand federal soldiers took place in the afternoon and on into the night.

While these federal troops were destroying the Fontaine's beautiful Fontainebleau, Sarah Aylett Fontaine and her two daughters made their way to the third floor of the house and locked themselves in a room. Although they could hear most of what was happening, they felt somewhat safe locked in that room. As the hours went on they could hear the laughter and cursing of the men that called themselves soldiers.

General George Washington Getty was the man that was in command of these fourteen thousand federal troops. General Getty had set up camp on the Fontaine's plantation less than a mile from the Fontaine's main house. There is no way that this general could not have heard what was happening at Fontainebleau, and he could surely see the smoke from all the buildings that were burning and the smoke from the pits that were dug to cook the slaughtered animals.

As the terrifying hours went on, sometime after midnight two of Mr. Fontaine's slaves, Beverley and Braxton, made their way to the third floor, where Sarah and her daughters had locked themselves in a room. The two male slaves told their mistress that they thought it best for her and her two daughters to try to make their way to the next plantation.

Sarah felt that might be the best thing to do. With no one there on the plantation except herself, her daughters, and her slaves, she decided to try to escape and make it through the woods to Colonel Carter's plantation. The two male slaves, Beverly and Braxton, told their mistress to try to sneak down the back staircase to the back door and go through the flower garden. They told Sarah that they and several other male slaves would be in the lower part of the flower garden.

They would be there waiting for her and her daughters, armed with axes in case any of the federal soldiers saw them. With fear running through all of them, Sarah and her daughters softly and quietly made their way from the third floor of their home to the flower garden. Sarah knew that if any of the soldiers saw them that they would probably rape and kill them, and she knew that it probably would not be a quick death.

While Sarah quickly made her way through the flower garden with her daughters directly behind her, she could see out of the corner of her eye glimpses of some of her slaves there to defend her. As she was reaching the end of her garden, one of the male slaves whispered, "Miss Sarah, go up the ravine that heads to the big woods." As Sarah and her children trampled through the woods, tangling themselves in the thickets and underbrush, she thought they would never make it to Colonel Carter's plantation. Sarah and her daughters had never been exposed to such harsh conditions, but she knew that if they were to live that they had to make it somehow. After two miles through the woods they finally made it to the Carter plantation. It was almost daylight when they arrived.

When they reached Pampatike, the home of Colonel Carter, Sarah and her children were exhausted. The Fontaines stayed with the Carters for a day or two before returning to their home. When they returned they found nothing but total destruction. The main house was not burned and was still standing, but everything else was gone. The Fontaine family had lost everything they had worked to have for so many years. Mr. Fontaine's "model farm" was gone, and there were no livestock, not even a chicken.

When William Spotswood Fontaine returned after visiting his sick mother he found his plantation in ruins. They had no choice but to load what little they had into wagons and go to his mother's farm in Henry County. The Fontaines stayed in Henry County for about a year before moving to Greensboro, North Carolina. William Fontaine sold his Fontainebleau home and bought a little cottage in Greensboro and named it Everhope.

Sarah and her family only stayed in Greensboro for two years before returning to Virginia. They moved to Accomac County, where William Fontaine became president of a school for girls known as Atlantic Female College. Sarah, William, and her daughter Sarah stayed in the county for a few years. Marion had married while living in Greensboro to her cousin, John Hairson Redd, and had moved back

Marian Fontaine Redd

Sarah Fontaine Sampson

to Henry County, Virginia. After their daughter, Sarah, married Henry Sampson in 1873, William and Sarah moved to Texas to be with their son. But, only after two years in Texas, Sarah Aylett Fontaine became ill, so the Fontaines decided to move to Reidsville, North Carolina, where there youngest son lived.

But, Sarah's health did not get better. Sarah Aylett Fontaine died March 5, 1876, in Reidsville, North Carolina. After Sarah's death, William lived with his son there in Reidsville. Before William's death he had made several trips to his home in Virginia. William Spotswood Fontaine died July 13,1882 in Reidsville.

XV
PHILIP AYLETT JR. (1791-1848)

General Aylett was a grandson of Sarah Shelton Henry. His mother, Elizabeth Henry, was the youngest daughter of Sarah. He had a sister who also lived in King William County, Virginia. She was Sarah Shelton Aylett, who married William Spotswood Fontaine. So many of the family lived in the King William area. He attended the University of Virginia, like his brothers and many cousins.

He served in the Virginia State Militia. Later, he married Judith Page Waller. He later had two sons, Patrick Henry Aylett and William Roane Aylett, who would become very successful lawyers and very distinguished gentlemen, like their father.

Patrick Henry Aylett was born in 1825. He had attended Rumford Academy, Washington College, and University of Virginia. He would later graduate from Harvard College. Mr. Aylett was practicing law in Virginia when his father, General Aylett, died. Mr. Aylett moved back to King William County and lived in the family home, Montville. Montville had been left to him after his father's death. He practiced law there in the county until 1853, but decided to move back to Richmond, where he married Emily Rutherford.

But, in 1870 there was a disaster that struck. He was in the supreme courtroom on the second floor when the floor collapsed. It killed a number of people, including Patrick Henry Aylett. Mr. Aylett was a very distinguished lawyer and was greatly admired by all. Patrick

Henry Aylett left a wife and three daughters. These three daughters would later marry and become ladies of high social standing.

General Aylett had another son, Colonel William Roane Aylett, who was born in 1833. He, too, would become a successful lawyer. He also attended Rumford Academy and University of Virginia. In 1860, he married Alice Brockenbrough. But, when the Civil War began, he enlisted. He was ask to raise a company of volunteers. They were named Taylor Grays. Mr. William Aylett quickly moved to captain, then major, and later colonel. He fought in many, many battles. He was wounded in 1863 at Gettysburg, at Peachtree Hill. In the winter of 1864, his command was confined to the trenches in the Bermuda Hundreds area of Virginia. They were there for nine months. They were exposed to the harsh winter without much shelter and in the summer were sometimes left with no water.

Colonel Aylett only left his command one time, and that was because his wife was very sick. He was gone only a short time. When the war was over he returned to his home, Montville, to find his farm in ruins and his family almost starving. Colonel Aylett had moved back to the family home after his brother had moved to Richmond. He started practicing law again and worked to get food for his family and to somewhat restore his farm. He raised and educated his children and became the lawyer for King William County for seventeen years.

In 1895, his wife Alice fell down the cellar stairs and suffered a brain concussion. She died a few days later. Colonel William Roane Aylett died in January of 1900, a day after suffering a stroke. They were both buried in the Aylett family cemetery, but later, when the road was widened, their graves were moved to Saint David's church in the Aylett community.

Patrick Henry Aylett and William Roane Aylett were great-grandsons that Sarah Shelton Henry would have been very proud of, like so many of her grandsons and other great-grandsons.

William Roane Aylett

XVI
WILLIAM WINSTON
FONTAINE (1834-1917)

William was a great-grandson of Sarah Shelton Henry through her daughter, Elizebeth. William's parents were William Spotswood Fontaine and Sarah Shelton Aylett. William Winston Fontaine was born at Montville, the home of his maternal grandparents, but was raised at his family home, Fontainebleau. Like so many other children during the colonial period, William was tutored at home during the first few years.

Later, he was sent to Rumford Military School to prepare him for college. He then attended the University of Virginia in Charlottesville for several years. He had studied law, like some of his first cousins, but didn't think becoming a lawyer was something he wanted to do. He was so disinterested that he did not take the bar exam.

After college, William Winston Fontaine taught school in the village of Aylett for a few years before accepting a position as a teacher at Pegram School in Richmond, Virginia. This was during the early 1860s. He was living in the Mechanics Institute Building, where the Secession Convention would hold their sessions. William Winston Fontaine was very interested in what was taking place and what was to come.

William enlisted in the Civil War in March of 1861. In April of 1861 his company went into regular service, but before leaving,

William married Mary Adelaide Burrows in her home in Richmond. She was the daughter of Reverend John Lansing Burrows.

In March of 1862, while still serving in the Civil War, William contracted typhoid fever and was sent to his home, Fontainebleau, in King William County, Virginia. He attempted to return to duty only after a few weeks, but fell unconscious and was taken back to his father's home. He stayed there for many weeks and was at the point of death. He did not return to duty until June of 1862.

When William Winston Fontaine returned to his home, Fontainebleau, after the war, he found the home had been vandalized by federal troops. The plantation was destroyed; nothing was left. The main house was still standing, but nothing else. His father's "model farm" was gone. This plantation had once been one of the most beautiful plantations in Virginia. His parents had left after the destruction of their plantation and were living in Greensboro, North Carolina. William did not go to Greensboro. With no money, and homeless, he knew he had to find a home and some way of making a living for his family. He took his family to Fredericksburg, Virginia, in hopes of starting a new life.

After moving to Fredericksburg, William Winston Fontaine somehow opened a school for young girls. It was called Spotswood Female Academy. He remained at the school a number of years before accepting a position as president of Port Sullivan College in Texas. He later became president of Baylor University and later moved to Austin, Texas, where he established another school.

In 1880, William Winston Fontaine moved his family to Louisville, Kentucky, because of his wife's bad health. He excepted another presidency at Holyoke Academy there in Louisville, but in 1887 his wife died and later William moved back to Austin, Texas, to become a professor at the University of Texas there in Austin. William stayed at the

University of Texas for a number of years before retiring.

After retiring, he moved to Galveston, Texas, before moving to Mississippi to live with his daughter. Not only was William Winston Fontaine a scholar, but also a poet. It is said that his beliefs and style were those of a "nineteenth century southern romanticist."

He contributed articles to Virginia Historical Magazine and the William & Mary Quarterly Magazine on genealogy, Virginia history, and a number of other historical subjects. While living in Louisville, Kentucky, he served as an editor and a writer for a Confederate veterans magazine. A number of his poems were published in Virginia newspapers, other southern magazines, and later published in the London Times and other British magazines.

His younger sister, Sarah Spotswood Fontaine Sampson, was an accomplished scholar, writer, and poet. His father, William Spotswood Fontaine, was also an accomplished writer, among many of his talents.

William Winston Fontaine died in 1917 at the home of his daughter, May Aylett Fontaine Borum. He is buried in Mississippi with other family members.

William Winston Fontaine
1834- 1917

XVII
PATRICK HENRY FONTAINE (1841-1915)

Patrick Henry Fontaine was another great-grandson of Sarah Shelton Henry. His parents were also William Spotswood Fontaine and Sarah Shelton Aylett. He was born in 1841 at the family home, Fontainebleau, in King William County, Virginia. He was a very handsome man and stood six feet tall. It was noted that his spirit showed the good "breeding" of all his ancestors.

He, like his brother, was also taught school at an early age in the family home. When he was ten years old he was sent to Rumford Military School there in King William County, Virginia, to continue his education. He later attended the University of Virginia before going into the Civil War.

At an early age of fourteen he was baptized, and only five years later was preaching his first sermon at nineteen years old. He knew that was the path he wanted to take and devote his life to, and he did until his death in 1915.

When he entered the Civil War he was first lieutenant of Carter's battery of King William County. That was June of 1861. In the spring of 1862, his brother Phillip came down with typhoid fever or malaria and died in a Richmond hospital before their father, William Spotswood Fontaine, could get there. Phillip's body was brought back to his home, Fontainebleau, and buried in the flower garden.

After being discharged from the army for a while, Patrick Henry Fontaine taught school and spent his time studying the ministry. His father, William Spotswood Fontaine, who was also a minister, helped Patrick with his studies. In September of 1863 his hard work paid off—he was ordained as a Baptist minister at Colasse Church in King William County, Virginia.

Patrick Henry Fontaine's first cousin, Phillip Aylett, was the commander of the 53rd Virginia Infantry Regiment. He appointed his first cousin, Patrick, as captain and chaplin of the regiment. Patrick was in this position from September 1863 to April 1865. Not only did he preach to the soldiers, but he also helped the surgeons with the wounded.

His fiancee, Annie Elizabeth Redd, who was also a first cousin, was attending school in Charlotte, North Carolina, in February of 1865. She was attending Melrose Female College. She was living with an older sister who had married into the Caldwell family. The Caldwells were living in a large, three-story house that had been built in 1774. The historic house would later become the Charlotte History Museum.

Patrick Henry Fontaine decided it would be best for he and Annie to marry right away instead of waiting until June. Patrick knew General Sherman was on his way to Charlotte. Patrick took a few days off and went to Charlotte to get Annie. Most people in Charlotte were taking what they could and leaving before General Sherman got there. Annie, not prepared for a wedding, had to borrow a dress from her sister. It was a beautiful blue silk dress.

Patrick and Annie boarded a train to Greensboro, North Carolina, to be married by Patrick's father, William Spotswood Fontaine. It was a rough and uncomfortable train ride, but they made it to Greensboro and were married on February 23, 1865. Patrick had to leave the next day to return to the army. Patrick's parents had moved to Greensboro after their plantation home, Fontainebleau, was destroyed by federal troops. The Fontaines called their little house in Greensboro Everhope.

After the war ended in 1865 Patrick returned to Greensboro and continued to live there for fourteen years. His parents moved back to Virginia for a while. Times were very hard for all southerners after the war. Patrick began preaching wherever he could. There was no money because the church was in poverty, like everyone was. There was a little farm of fifty acres that had come with the little house. Since there was no money in teaching or preaching, Patrick Henry Fontaine had to do something to feed his family.

He thought of the idea of covering the vegetable bed with a white cloth in late winter so the planted seeds could get about a month's start in the ground. No one had ever done that. A few years later someone claimed they had discovered the idea and tried to get a patent on the idea, but Mr. Fontaine produced a magazine and some newspaper articles to prove he was the one who had discovered the covered plant bed.

Mr. Fontaine continued growing and peddling his vegetables until a church in Reidsville asked him to be their minister. This was 1870 and Patrick's first paying job since the war had ended. He and his family stayed in the Greensboro-Reidsville area for twelve more years.

In 1883, the Fontaines moved to Halifax County, Virginia. Patrick would be the minister of five churches in the area. There, he bought his first home. It was called Elmo. It was a big house, with part of it having been built before the Revolutionary War.

Patrick Henry Fontaine was very educated in botany. He studied and enjoyed the habits of birds and insects. He spent a lot of time studying physical science. His father, William Spotswood Fontaine, also showed a great interest in botany.

Patrick enjoyed visiting with friends, and after dinner, lighting his pipe and talking about the Bible. He did not like liquor or anything to do with it. He was in prohibition camps in both Virginia and North Carolina.

Later, Patrick and his family moved to Person County, North Carolina. He bought another house near Woodsdale, but still kept his other house, Elmo. He lived in Person County for sixteen years before moving again to Granville County. He spent the last five years of his life preaching at Amis Chapel Baptist Church. Patrick and Annie lived in Bethel Hill.

Patrick Henry Fontaine and Annie Elizebeth Redd were married for fifty years. Close to the end of Patrick's life, at seventy-four years old, he was still riding horseback sometimes five to ten miles to one of his churches. On his last trip while riding through snow and rain he came down with influenza, which developed into pneumonia. He only lived a few days and died March 29, 1915.

There was said to have been close to a thousand people at the cemetery to show their respect to Mr. Fontaine. There were also some Croatan Indians at the cemetery who also wanted to show their respect to a friend and someone they admired. His wife, Annie, lived another twenty-one years there in their home.

Patrick Henry Fontaine was a man that was greatly admired by so many.

Patrick Henry Fontaine
1841-1915

XVIII
SARAH FONTAINE REDD
(1815-1909)

Sarah Fontaine Redd was a great-granddaughter of Sarah Shelton Henry. Her parents were William Winston Fontaine and Martha Hale Dandridge. Her grandmother was Martha Henry Fontaine, first child of Sarah Shelton Henry.

She was born in November of 1815 in Henry County, Virginia. She was raised on the Fontaine family farm on the Little Marrowbone Creek, not far from the Ridgeway, Virginia, area. She had two older brothers, William Spotswood Fontaine (1810-1882) and Patrick Henry Fontaine (1812-1845). William Spotswood Fontaine married Sarah Aylett and Patrick Henry Fontaine married Sarah Miller Cole.

Sarah Fontaine Redd's father, William Winston Fontaine, had traveled to the north Alabama territory to inspect some land. The land in the area was plentiful and cheap. Mr. Fontaine was a surveyor, as his father was. Mr. Fontaine and his slave, along with some other family members, wanted to travel to the area in hopes of buying some land and moving their families there.

But, on the trip back, Mr. Fontaine and his slave ran into some bad weather. They were traveling horseback and did not have much means of any shelter from the cold rain. William Winston Fontaine obviously was sick with pneumonia and died at their campsite. They had set up their campsite close to the Abington, Virginia, area. Mr.

Fontaine's slave buried his master beside the creek before making his way back to the Fontaine farm. His loyal slave brought Mr. Fontaine's horse and supplies back with him.

Mr. Fontaine's wife, Martha, was left with three small children to raise. She was just twenty-one years old herself. Sarah Fontaine Redd was only a baby when her father died. Martha Dandridge Fontaine raised her three children and ran the farm the best she could. Later, Sarah's older brother, Patrick Henry Fontaine, ran the farm. He later married and lived on his farm, which consisted of one hundred and twenty acres and five slaves. This was part of the original Leatherwood plantation. The Leatherwood plantation in Henry County, Virginia had belonged to his grandparents, Martha Henry and John Fontaine.

Patrick Henry Fontaine's father had inherited six hundred acres of the original Leatherwood plantation upon his father's death. His mother, Martha Henry Fontaine, had remained at Leatherwood until her death.

Sarah Fontaine Redd married when not quite sixteen years old. She married Edmund Burwell Redd. Edmund was from a good and wealthy family. When they married, they were given the plantation, Woodlawn, in Henry County, Virginia. Woodlawn was owned by Edmund's father, John Redd. The plantation also sat on the Morrowbone Creek.

But, Edmund Redd was a bad husband and father. Before he had married Miss Fontaine, he had attended the University of North Carolina and the University of Virginia, but he was dismissed.

Mr. Redd obviously had an alcohol problem. Sarah Fontaine Redd and her children were mostly supported by her father-in-law, John Redd.

Edmund Redd died in 1850 of what was described as, "a drunkard's death." Sarah was left to raise nine children. She also had to maintain the farm and care for her twelve slaves. She did raise her children and raised them well. One of her sons, John Hairston Redd, married his first cousin, Marion Dandridge Fontaine, daughter of Sarah Redd's brother, William. John became a doctor. There are no known children born to John and Marian.

Sarah Fontaine Redd died on February 16, 1909, at the home of a granddaughter. She is buried in the city cemetery in Reidsville, North Carolina. There are also a number of family members buried in that cemetery.

Sarah was ninety-three years old when she died. She still played the piano and read everyday. She was lucky enough to have lived to see eight generations of her family. References say she was a very good person, and that she did whatever it took to educate her children and run her farm. She was also very kind to her slaves, and whenever they were sick she would give them their medicine herself and made sure they got whatever they needed. One of her daughters told the story of how she and her mother, Sarah, would walk down to the slave cabins each time the slaves would have a celebration. The daughter said that all the slaves were happy to see "Miss Sarah" had come to join them in their celebration.

Sarah Fontaine Redd left many descendants that I'm sure had many, many stories to tell.

IXX
SPENCER ROANE THORPE
(1842-1902)

Spencer Roane Thorpe was the son of Thomas Thorpe and Sarah Anne Roane. Sarah Anne Roane was a great-granddaughter of Sarah Shelton and Patrick Henry. Her father, Fayette Roane, was the son of Sarah Shelton's second daughter, Anne Henry Roane.

Spencer was born in Louisville, Kentucky, in 1842, but lived most of his childhood in the Bardstown, Kentucky, area. He was educated at St. Joseph College. He enlisted in the Civil War at a young age in December of 1861. He was wounded at the battle of Drainsville, Virginia, but he was quickly promoted to first lieutenant. He was in command of four companies. In July of 1863 he was seriously wounded at Corydon and left for dead. He was taken prisoner and sent to Johnson's Island. He stayed there until October of 1864. He was later discharged as a captain.

In 1867 he moved to Louisiana and was a very successful lawyer, but a few years later he went to the Ventura, California, area and saw great possibilities. Not long after his trip to California he returned to Louisiana and closed his business. By 1883 he had returned to the Ventura, California, area. He had married Helena Barbin while still living in Louisiana.

Mr. Thorpe spent most of his time at his various properties, and by 1889 he had moved his family to what is now Los Angeles, California

Mr. Thorpe lived in Los Angeles till his death in 1905. He had gone to one of his ranches to oversee the harvesting, but as he was riding from the ranch to the Simi Valley he apparently had a heart attack and died on the side of the road. When Mr. Thorpe's horse came back with no rider, they knew something had happened to him.

Spencer Roane Thorpe had been very successful in his sixty-three years. He was among a list of descendants of Sarah Shelton and Patrick Henry who had made their mark in history.

Spencer Roane Thrope
1842-1905

XX

DAVID SHELTON (1736-1800)

David Shelton is my direct ancestor from the Hanover County Sheltons. David was a brother of Sarah Shelton Henry. He was also born and raised at the Shelton home, Rural Plains. After leaving Rural Plains, David lived on the Virginia and North Carolina county line. His first wife was Elizabeth Matlock. There were three children from this marriage.

After his first wife's death he married Susannah Vaughn, the mother of my great-great-great-grandfather, David Valentine Shelton. David and Susannah were married on June 3, 1784. There were five children born to that marriage.

Sarah Henry's brother, David, was appointed sheriff of Caswell County, North Carolina, in 1777, and later was appointed the county treasurer. He was appointed again to serve as sheriff until 1785. He was also appointed tax appraiser.

David and his family's plantation home was in Locust Hill on Shelton Creek in Caswell County, North Carolina. This land was part of a grant from his father, John Shelton. This land later became part of North Carolina.

This David Shelton owned hundreds of parcels of land in North Carolina and what would later became the state of Tennessee.

David Shelton's will was written on March 31, 1800. His wife, Susannah, was left with young children. Susannah later married a

Godfrey Crowder and moved to Mecklenberg County, Virginia. Most of her children went with her, including my great-great-great-grandfather, David Valentine Shelton.

David Valentine Shelton later married Anne Baker and lived his life in Mecklenberg County, Virginia. He had a very successful life and had five sons to live a long productive life. One of those sons was my great-great-grandfather, Dr.John B. Shelton, who became a doctor like his older brother, Dr. James Shelton. David Shelton left the Shelton plantation and many tracts of land to his youngest son, Henry Shelton, who would later marry and have a family; some research shows that he had four children, then left that wife and children and moved to Lumpkin County, Georgia, probably in hopes of finding gold. There was gold in the north Georgia mountains at that time. Henry Shelton later remarried and started a new family in Georgia. He had already sold many acres of his father's land in Caswell County before leaving for Lumpkin County, Georgia.

Sarah Shelton Henry's brother, David Shelton, played a very important part in the development of Caswell County, North Carolina. I have never found any type of portrait of David Shelton or his wife, Susannah Vaughn, but I was pleased to find a picture of David Shelton's house in the Locust Hill area of Caswell County, North Carolina. The picture was taken many years after his death. The picture shows where stucco was added to the outside walls long after David Shelton's death.

Research shows that one of Sarah Shelton Henry's brothers did visit Sarah's home, Scotchtown. I would like to think that brother was David Shelton, my direct ancestor.

Shelton House
Caswell co, NC

Shelton House
Caswell co, NC

XXI
SOME NEPHEWS AND GREAT-NEPHEWS

John Shelton (1755-1843) was a nephew of Sarah Shelton Henry. John was the first child born to Sarah's brother, David Shelton, and his first wife, Elizabeth Matlock. John was born while David and Elizabeth were still living in the Louisa and Hanover County, Virginia, area.

John was a soldier in the Revolutionary War. He enlisted from Hanover County. He fought in the Battle of Valley Forge. John's father, David Shelton, was also in the Revolutionary War. John's father later moved to Caswell County, North Carolina. After the war, John Shelton married Susannah Bradley, daughter of James Bradley, also of Caswell County, North Carolina.

John Shelton, his family, and the Bradley family moved to an area that would later become Tennessee. This area was still in the state of North Carolina when they moved. The Sheltons built a house before 1796. This house was made of rock and stone. The house would later be known as "The Old Rock House" or "The Shelton Rock House." The rock house was still standing till 1935. The rock and stone had begun to crumble so it was demolished by the owners.

The county had been divided by 1935 and was at that time in Trousdale County, close to Hartsville, Tennessee. John Shelton and Susannah Bradley had seven known children. One of their sons moved to the state of Kentucky, one moved to another part of Tennessee, one had married a Rebecca Dickerason and left a large number of descendants, and one daughter, Blanche, married a Mr. Whiteside. They left a number of Whiteside descendants that stayed in the Sumner, Smith, and Trousdale area of Tennessee.

Some research shows that John Shelton, son of David Shelton of Caswell County, North Carolina, died in 1843 in Sumner County, Tennessee.

Bradley House
Sumner co, TN

James Shelton (1786-1850) was also a nephew of Sarah Shelton Henry. He was the second child born to Sarah's brother, David, and his second wife, Susannah Vaughn. James was a brother of my great-great-great-grandfather, David Valentine Shelton of Caswell County, North Carolina and later Mecklenburg County, Virginia.

James married Nancy Marshall, daughter of William Marshall and Lucy Goode. Nancy's grandparents were Bennett Goode and Martha Jefferson, aunt of President Thomas Jefferson.

There were nine known children born to James and Nancy Shelton. James and his wife had settled on the present-day highway 70, a little east of Lebanon, Tennessee. This was land that is now at the Smith-Wilson county line. This was land that was owned by James's father, David Shelton of Caswell County, North Carolina. All of that area was at that time was in the state of North Carolina. James's father owned hundred and hundreds of acres of land in the surrounding area.

The Shelton's first known child to die was William (1820-1821). The second known child to die was Susan or Susannah (1816-1831), named after James's mother, Susannah Vaughn Shelton. Both children, along with other Sheltons, are buried in the Shelton Cemetery on the original Shelton land on highway 70 in Wison county Tennessee. The cemetery is known now as the Shelton-Link cemetery. Obviously at some point, a Link family owned the Shelton land. This area was known as Round Lick.

One of James and Nancy Shelton's sons was David (1813-1886). David had a very full life. He attended school close to his home, but later graduated from the University of Nashville in Nashville, Tennessee. He had a degree in law and set up his practice in Jackson, Mississippi. David later married Miss Levinia Lea.

By the time the Civil War broke out, this David Shelton had acquired a lot of land. He was living on the outskirts of Jackson,

Mississippi. Jackson, Mississippi, was hit hard during the Civil War. Mr. Shelton's home was burnt to the ground.

David Shelton is buried in the Greenwood cemetery in Jackson, Mississippi.

Another son of James and Nancy Shelton was William (1824-1910). This son also graduated from the University of Nashville. He graduated with a degree in theology. He also attended Hamilton University in New York. Mr. Shelton was a preacher, teacher, and a professor of Greek and Latin.

He was president of a number of universities across the country. He was also a preacher in Clarksville, Tennessee. Mr Shelton married Miss Virginia Campbell and had eight children. Mr.Shelton died at the home of his daughter, Nannie Shelton McClary. He is buried in Buffalo Springs cemetery in Stanford, Kentucky.

One of James Shelton and Nancy Marshall's daughters, Lucy Goode Shelton, married Dr. James Dearing Whiteside. Dr. Whiteside not only practiced medicine but also had a snuff factory in Wilson County, Tennessee. They lived in a brick house in Wilson County. It was one of the first brick houses built in the area. Their home was called Vintage.

Another daughter of James Shelton, Martha Goode Shelton, was married to Haywood Riddle. Mr. Riddle was very politically active.

James Shelton of Wilson County, Tennessee, died in 1850 and was buried in his family cemetery on what was the James Shelton plantation. The cemetery and what was his original land sits on highway 70, which runs through the counties of Smith and Wison in Tennessee.

Another nephew of Sarah's who was born many years after Sarah's death was Henry Shelton (1791-1880). He was also a son of Sarah's brother, David. He was the last child born to Sarah's brother, David, and his wife, Susannah Vaughn. Henry was only nine years old when his father, David, died. Henry inherited a large portion of his father's estate. He was also left the house that sat on County Line Creek in Caswell County, North Carolina, the house was where all of Sarah's brother's children by his second marriage were born. Henry Shelton was a very educated man who spoke fluent Latin. He married Temperence Harris in 1815. There were two sons and at least two daughters born to Henry Shelton before he left Caswell County, North Carolina.

Henry was mostly listed as a distiller while still living in Caswell County, North Carolina, but by 1828 Henry Shelton had disappeared from the county. Around 1835, Henry Shelton showed up in the Georgia mountains. He had married again and was raising his second family.

As to why he left Caswell County, North Carolina, and moved to the Georgia mountains, it is uncertain. Some speculate that it was due to gambling debts. As early as 1817 he had sold 369 acres of land that sat on County Line Creek to a Romulus Sanders. The deed shows that his track of land was on the main road next to Nicolas Matlock. Henry Shelton's father's first wife was Elizabeth Matlock. For what ever reason, this nephew of Sarah Shelton Henry did leave his home in Caswell County, North Carolina.

Henry Shelton died on November 26, 1880, at his home in the Georgia mountains. In a newspaper article that was written about one of his daughters by his second marriage, she stated that she was very young when her father died but she did remember he had been a teacher in a one-room schoolhouse. Henry Shelton left many descendants from his second family.

My great-great-grandfather, Dr. John Bullock Shelton (1824-1883) was a great nephew of Sarah Shelton Henry. He was raised at his home, Rebel Hill, in Buffalo Springs Virginia. This was approximately eightly miles from Richmond, Virginia. He was one of six sons born to David Valentine Shelton and Anne Baker of Mecklenburg County, Virginia. Dr. John, like his older brother, Dr. James, graduated from the University of Pennsylvania with a degree in medicine.

Dr James Shelton
1822- 1898

Dr. John B Shelton
1824 - 1883

Both Dr. John B. and Dr. James graduated from Randolph Macon school when it was still in Boydton, Virginia. Later the school moved to Ashland, Virginia, which is only about fifteen miles from Sarah Shelton Henry's last home, Scotchtown.

After graduating from medical school, Dr. John B. Shelton came back to his home, Rebel Hill, for a few years before leaving for McNairy County, Tennessee. The area he settled in was called Rose Creek. The little community of Rose Creek in McNairy County, Tennessee, was just off the present-day highway 64.

Dr. Shelton took with him a female slave named Emma. Dr. Shelton and Emma arrived in Tennessee around 1854. Dr. Shelton and Emma had a daughter named Lucy, who was born in April of 1857. Dr Shelton did not marry till February 1859.

Dr. John B. Shelton married Jane Elvira Duke in Rose Creek, Tennessee. The Duke family had arrived in McNairy County a number of years earlier. The Duke family was from the Goochland, Louisa County, Virginia, area.

The Sheltons stayed in McNairy County, Tennessee, till the spring of 1862, before traveling to Arkansas County, Arkansas, to start a new life. The Civil War had begun and was very active in the area they were living in. They were very close to where the Battle of Shiloh was taking place—one of the bloodiest battles of the war. The Sheltons traveled to their new home when my greatgrandfather, David Duke Shelton, was about nine to ten months old. He was born June of 1861.

In the spring of 1862, the Sheltons, Emma, and her daughter, Lucy, traveled to an area across the Mississippi River, far from Virginia, where Dr. Shelton and Jane Duke had been born and raised. The Sheltons, Emma, and Lucy all remained close until their deaths. After Dr. Shelton and his wife, Jane, died, Emma moved into the Shelton house and raised the five youngest children of Dr. Shelton

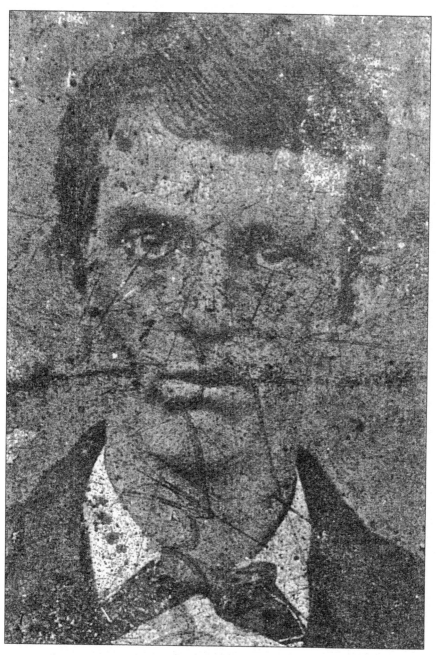

David Duke Shelton
1861-1906

David Duke Shelton
Family ca: 1904

Descendants of :
David Duke Shelton
Ca: 1942

and Jane Duke.

When Lucy married, she named her first daughter after the Shelton's oldest child Ida. Ida and Lucy were half sisters. Lucy and her family lived next door to the Sheltons for a number of years before moving to the Duke plantation, were her husband worked. This was Jane Duke Shelton's parents' plantation. Ida Shelton said Lucy was the prettiest bride she had ever seen.

A number of years ago I had the pleasure of meeting one of Lucy's granddaughters, Elfreda Montgomery Oakes. Mrs. Oakes was in her eighties at the time. She said she had a picture of her grandmother, Lucy, but her daughter had borrowed it to make a copy. I never had another opportunity to meet with Mrs. Oakes or to see Lucy's picture.

Dr. Shelton and his wife, Jane Duke, are buried in an area where my Shelton grandparents and my mother, Norma Jean Shelton Phelps, is buried. Emma Shelton, Dr. Shelton's slave, is also buried in the area, in a cemetery that was on Shelton land.

Another great nephew of Sarah Henry was Jesse Harper Shelton, a brother of my great-great grandfather. Harper also attended Randolph Macon College, like his two older brothers. He became a lawyer and moved to Sussex County, Virginia, where he spent the rest of his life.

He also taught school at Coppahaunk Springs, not far from his home. He enlisted in the Civil War in May of 1861. He was in the 41st Virginia Infantry Sussex Sharpshooters.

In 1866 he became judge of the county clerk of Sussex County, Virginia. Later, in the 1880s, he began teaching school again. Jesse Harper Shelton married Louise Land and they had a number of children, one being Maggie Shelton Stephenson.

Norma Shelton Phelps
1927 - 1958

Granddaughter and Great grandchildren of
David Duke Shelton
1951

Judge Jesse Harper Shelton
1826- 1909

David Shelton
1828- 1913

Judge Harper Shelton died on December 14,1909. He is buried in the Montrose cemetery not far from his home.

William Dozier Shelton was also a brother of my great-great grandfather. He was the last child born to my great-great-great grandparents in Mecklenburg County, Virginia. He was born in 1836.

He also enlisted in the Civil War. He joined the Clarksville Blues in Clarksville, Virginia. He was a major by the end of the war. Major Shelton and the remaining few in his regiment were at Appomattox when General Lee surrendered.

After the war, William Dozier Shelton married Susan Crowder, also of Mecklenburg County, Virginia. They had at least eight known children. Mr. Shelton spent the rest of his life after the war raising tobacco.

I visited Mr. Shelton's old homeplace a number of years ago. The only thing that was still standing was a small barn and what looked to be an old tobacco barn. You could tell where the house would have been. There was a small Shelton cemetery not far from where the house once stood. This is where William Dozier Shelton, his wife, Susan, and a few of his children are buried. His daughter, Sallie S. Shelton, is also buried there. She moved back to her family farmhouse after retiring. She had lived in Richmond for a number of years. She lived in the old house until it burned in 1985. She lived to be 104 years old.

Maj. William Dozier Shelton
1836- 1913.

XXII
ANGES SHELTON SUTHERLAND (1757-1821)

Anges was a niece of Sarah Shelton Henry. She was a daughter of Sarah's brother, David, and his first wife, Elizabeth Matlock. Anges married John Sutherland and lived in what is now the Danville, Virginia area. This was very close to her father's plantation in Locust Hill, Caswell County, North Carolina.

In 1805, Anges and her family moved to what is now east Tennessee. It was very close to the present day Knoxville, Tennessee. They lived on the Clinch River, where her husband ran a ferry.

She had two sons, George and John Jr. John Jr., as a young man, worked as a clerk in Knoxville. But for some reason, in 1824, Agnes and her family decided to move to Decatur, Alabama. The two sons opened up a merchandising store. They would ride quite a distance to get supplies to sell in their store, but the store did not have much success. Her son, George, was disappointed and decided to move to Austin, Texas.

Her son, John Sutherland Jr., decided he wanted to be a doctor. He practiced there in the Decatur, Alabama, area while keeping his merchandising store open. But by 1835, Dr. Sutherland had also moved to Austin, Texas. Dr. Sutherland liked that area and decided he wanted to make that his home, so by 1837 he had closed his Alabama business and move to an area call Egypt, Texas.

Dr. Sutherland built a home on the west side of the Colorado River. Dr. John Sutherland was also a doctor at the Alamo. He did not fight in the battle at the Alamo, but was there to help those that were wounded and to do surgery on those who needed it. Dr. Sutherland's nephew, son of his brother, George, did fight in the battle at the Alamo and was also a medical assistant at the Alamo. His nephew was killed in the battle.

Dr. John Sutherland moved to Sulpher Springs, Texas, and was the founder of the first post office in the area. He would open his home to travelers, the homeless, and those in need. He was known as a good Christian man.

Dr. Sutherland's grandfather, David Shelton of Caswell County, North Carolina, had requested that his grandson, John Sutherland, sell Shelton land in what is now Tennessee and Kentucky. Dr. John Sutherland died in 1867. Dr. Sutherland's grandaughter, Annie B. Sutherland, published her grandfather's work "The Fall of the Alamo," in 1936.

Sarah Shelton Henry had quite a few in her extended family that were very successful in whatever path they decided to take.

Dr. John Sutherland
1792- 1867

XXIII
DAVID V. SHELTON'S REBEL HILL, BUFFALO SPRINGS, VIRGINIA

Sarah Shelton Henry had a nephew, who was my great-great-great-grandfather, David Valentine Shelton (1789-1864). He was the son of Sarah's brother, David Shelton, and his wife, Susannah Vaughn. David Valentine Shelton was married to Anne Baker. Their plantation, Rebel Hill, was a natural springs resort for health and entertainment. In the pre-Civil War days, Buffalo Springs plantation was self-sustaining. The vegetables for the dining room were grown in the plantation gardens and the meat was raised on the plantation's farms. The Shelton house was built in 1811. The original owner of the house was Ambrose Gregory.

The house had been described as having paneled wainscoting upstairs and down. The house originally had ingle closets before being restored in 1941. In 1818, Shelton's brother-in-law, Joseph Speed, owned the property and operated a tavern at the resort. From 1824 to 1828 Joseph Speed rented the natural springs resort to David Valentine Shelton. David Valentine Shelton and his family had lived in the town of Clarksville, a few miles from the resort, before moving to the natural springs resort in Buffalo Springs, Virginia. This house is at 105 Sixth Street in Clarksville, Virginia. It has had a few owners since the

Sheltons owned the house. Mr. Shelton owned the house from 1830 till 1833. The house was built around 1829 by John Bullock.

The Sheltons named their new house in Buffalo Springs, Rebel Hill. The house does sit on a hill, which now faces the highway. The plantation and the natural springs resort consisted of one hundred and sixty acres. The natural springs were thought to have been discovered in 1728 while surveying the Virginia and North Carolina line. In 1845 and 1846 the rate was one dollar a day for board, fifty cents for a meal, and half price for children and servants.

In 1849, David Valentine Shelton became sole owner of Buffalo Springs. Later, the dining room was remodeled to accommodate three to four hundred people. Shelton did have success with the resort for the next fourteen years. He was so confident of the spring's water that he would invite people to the resort to stay free of charge and pay later if cured.

The resort had a hotel, row cottages, a spring house, a number of outbuildings and the main house for the Sheltons. My great-great-grandfather, Dr. John Bullock Shelton, and his brothers were raised at the Shelton home, Rebel Hill. My great-great-grandfather returned to his home at Rebel Hill after graduating from the University of Pennsylvania for a few years before moving to Tennessee and later Arkansas when the Civil War had reached the part of Tennessee where he was living.

When the Civil War began, David Valentine Shelton wrote an advertisement in the local paper saying, "Families or individuals wishing to be removed from the scene of the war and its excitement will find a safe and pleasant retreat at Buffalo Springs." So many Virginia families were forced to leave their homes by the summer of 1861. The fighting was so intense nothing was safe. Many families did find refuge at Buffalo Springs. In the summer of 1861 the resort could accommodate four hundred people.

On one of my visits to Rebel Hill, and what was once a thriving natural spring resort, I sat on one of the small, rolling hills, trying to imagine how Buffalo Springs may have looked during the Shelton days. The only thing that remains is the original Shelton house that was restored in 1941 and a spring house that was been constructed after the state of Virginia brought the property.

David Valentine Shelton's father, David Shelton, was a brother of Sarah Shelton Henry. David Shelton's plantation and house was very close to what is now the Virginia and North Carolina state line. Sarah Shelton Henry's brother, David Shelton, lived on or near Shelton Creek in an area that was called Locust Hill.

David Valentine Shelton's mother was Susannah Vaughn of Caswell County, North Carolina. I would have thought that the initial V would have stood for his mother's maiden name, but it did not.

After David Valentine Shelton's death, his family Bible was in possession of my great-great-grandfather, Dr. John B. Shelton. In that Bible was written the birth date of David Valentine Shelton. It was February 14, 1789. At the time of his birth, Valentine's Day was not celebrated in this country, but in Rome it celebrated St. Valentine. The Sheltons were very educated men, so undoubtedly this is where David Valentine's father got the information.

When David Valentine Shelton became ill he sold his resort to Timothy Paxton. This was in December of 1863. David Valentine Shelton died January of 1864.

In 1867, the new owner made some improvements to Buffalo Springs. The war was over and the people were trying to get back to what was once a normal life. When Mr. Paxton reopened the natural springs resort, the fee was two dollars a day for board. As the years went on, the resort's name was changed to Lithia Springs. The spring water was sold in Paris and London. By 1885, the resort began showing signs of life like it once had when David Valentine Shelton owned the resort.

As the years passed, there were many names for the mineral spring water that passed through Mecklenburg County, Virginia. The state now owns the property and the Shelton house is still privately owned. On one of my visits to Buffalo Springs, Virginia, I met another descendant of David Valentine Shelton. It was Dr. William Shelton, who lived on the same highway about a mile or so from the Shelton home, Rebel Hill. Dr. William Shelton was a descendant of David Valentine Shelton's youngest son, William Dozier Shelton. Dr. Shelton invited me to his home that afternoon and was kind enough to share with me some old Shelton pictures and information that he had gathered through the years. Dr. William Shelton lived in a beautiful, old two-story house that was once part of the old Boydton College there in Boydton, Virginia. I had a wonderful afternoon talking to Dr. and Mrs. Shelton about our Shelton family. Dr. Shelton had given me directions to his great-grandfather's old farm and cemetery so I could walk around and take some pictures. The only things standing were two very old barns, probably tobacco barns .He said his great-grandfather raised tobacco after the Civil War.

Dr. William Shelton told me that he had always heard that David Valentine Shelton and his wife, Anne Baker, were buried directly across the highway from the Shelton house. This land would have been part of the Buffalo Springs resort at the time the Sheltons were buried there. He had also heard the story that there was an old man in the area that would take care of the graves of the Sheltons. I searched and searched and did not find anything to let me know this was where David Valentine Shelton and his wife Anne Baker were buried. I have later found that the old Shelton cemetery is in the woods behind an old church that sits on the highway. Of course, the highway would not have been there during the time the Sheltons owned Buffalo Springs. There are only three visible graves now: David V. Shelton, his wife, Anne, and a young son.

My great-grandfather, David Duke Shelton, son of Dr. John B. Shelton and Jane Elivia Duke, had an older sister, Ida Shelton Abbott, that I have been told would tell story after story about the Shelton families throughout history. These stories have been passed down generation after generation. One of her stories was about her grandfather's plantation, Rebel Hill.

David Valentine Shelton died the winter of 1864 and his wife, Anne Baker, died in 1870. The Shelton's house, Rebel Hill, still stands today and is beautiful. The back of the properly overlooks a natural spring that once was called spring number 2. This spring ran through the historical Buffalo Springs Resort and plantation.

David V. Shelton
and
Anne Baker

Shelton House
Date : unknown

Shelton House

XXIV

THE GRAVE

We are like the flowers of spring that stay dormant for a while and then break the soil to let us know of their existence. They let us know why they were here. They unfold each part of history though their descendants as the first flowers of spring unfold each petal, one at a time.

As each petal unfolds we learn more of who they were and who we are today. We not only resemble some of the physical characteristics of our ancestors, but the inner thoughts and feelings of those we never knew.

I do hope that was Sarah Shelton Henry in that unmarked, deserted, and forgotten grave that the archaeology team discovered a few years ago at Scotchtown of a woman that was buried over two hundred years ago. The location of this unmarked grave, just a few feet from the entrance into the cellar, gives me hope that it was Sarah. Again, I was told that their research did confirm it was a female . . . Sarah Shelton Henry is a woman that needs to be recognized for the woman she was. There was a lot more to Sarah than just being the first wife of Patrick Henry.

Whether Sarah suffered from postpartum depression or puerperal psychosis, a severe mental illness that can follow childbirth, or any form of mild to severe mental disorder after the birth of her last child, she still needs to be recognized. Sarah Shelton Henry was a good person from a good family. She didn't deserve to be treated as if in some way it was her fault, or treated as if she brought this illness upon herself and left in an unmarked grave in hopes no one would ever discover it. She was someone that was put in a cellar to live out her life in hopes the world would not find out. What a terrible situation the Henry family was put in so many years ago. I'm sure Patrick

Henry lived in fear that someone would find out that he was keeping his wife in the cellar of their home. I would think that Henry's dark secret haunted him everyday. What Patrick Henry and possibly the children had to do to keep this secret probably stayed in their minds and hearts until their deaths. There is no doubt in my mind, Sarah Shelton Henry did help her husband in her own way to become the great person that we all know today. Through his strength and endurance he changed the colony of Virginia, something we have known for over two hundred years. Now, it is time to know Sarah Shelton Henry, the beautiful, sweet, dark-haired girl that Patrick Henry took as his young bride in the Shelton home in 1754. I do hope that Patrick Henry did think often of Sarah and their short life together—a life that was brought to a sudden standstill when Sarah's mental health was so bad that it stopped everything that Sarah and Patrick had possibly dreamed of and ended with the bolting of Sarah's door until her death. She lived in that cold, damp cellar, waiting for a day to come when she could be with her children again, but that day never came. When it was all over, and all the sorrow and pain was gone, she still was treated as if she was nothing. She was put in an unmarked grave in hopes that no one would remember her or her years in the cellar. But we do remember. We remember how she was left there in an unmarked grave in the spring of 1775. Patrick Henry left Scotchtown later to start his new life in the governor's mansion in Williamsburg, Virginia. He and his children left behind a life that probably most of them wanted to forget. Hopefully, Sarah Shelton Henry's children did remember their mother and wanted to always cherish the good memories, but not forget how their mother suffered with her illness.

Whether or not Patrick Henry chose to remember Sarah or not is really not important. What is important is that Sarah Shelton Henry is not forgotten and will always be remembered as the sweet, dear girl, as she was referred to by Patrick Henry's mother so many, many years ago. Not long after Sarah's death, Patrick Henry married a young woman, was living in the governor's mansion, and making a change for the colony of Virginia. So, he may or may not have chosen to think about his life before he became the governor. Since Patrick Henry did not leave many documents about his life before moving to Williamsburg, how do we know he planted that lilac bush that Scotchtown refers to? There must have been some type of document written by Henry or possibly a letter from a family member for the archaeology team to do their research in that area. But, since the lilac bush would have had to be disturbed or removed, the team stopped their search.

I am sure there were many times that Patrick Henry stared at the dirt floor beneath his feet with a glazed look in his eyes and sorrow in his heart as he bolted Sarah's door. I wonder if he knew that Sarah's cries from the cellar would be heard many, many years later.

I hope that in the future an archaeology team will be asked again to come to Scotchtown to reinvestigate that area where the remains of that female were found. Maybe then we will know if that is where Patrick Henry left his wife. After all, Sarah Shelton Henry was the mistress of Scotchtown. It is where she had her last child and where she lived the last three to four years of her life. It may have been in the cellar, but it was her home.

Then, maybe Sarah Shelton Henry can finally be at peace and get the liberty that she so well deserves. She has waited over two hundred years for that.

CPSIA information can be obtained
at www.ICGtesting.com
Printed in the USA
BVOW08s1324050418
512462BV00003B/313/P